Language Essentials for Teachers of R<

MW01000216

Module 5

Getting Up to Speed: Developing Fluency

Second Edition

Louisa C. Moats, Ed.D.

Marcia Davidson, Ph.D.

Presenter's Kit by Carol Tolman, Ed.D.

Sopris West®
EDUCATIONAL SERVICES

A Cambium Learning® Company

BOSTON, MA · LONGMONT, CO

Printed in the United States of America
Published and Distributed by

Sopris West®
EDUCATIONAL SERVICES

A Cambium Learning® Company

4093 Specialty Place • Longmont, Colorado 80504
(303) 651-2829 • www.soprislearning.com

How does copyright pertain to LETRS® Module 5?

Dedication

To my husband, Steve Mitchell, whose unwavering support makes LETRS possible.

—LCM

To my children—Ben, Andy, and Pete—who are my sources of inspiration. And a special thanks to Louisa Moats, who has so generously and graciously taught me so much about teaching and learning.

—MD

Acknowledgments

LETRS® modules have been developed with the help of many people. The national LETRS trainers—including Carol Tolman, Mary Dahlgren, Nancy Hennessy, Susan Hall, Marcia Davidson, Deb Glaser, Linda Farrell, Judi Dodson, Pat Sekel, Joan Sedita, Anthony Fierro, and Anne Whitney—have offered valuable suggestions for improving module content and structure. Their commitment to delivering LETRS across the country is appreciated beyond measure.

Bruce Rosow, Kevin Feldman, Susan Lowell, Patricia Mathes, Marianne Steverson, Lynn Kuhn, Jan Hasbrouck, Marsha Berger, Susan Smartt, and Nancy Eberhardt contributed their expertise to LETRS first edition modules and often provide valuable input and feedback. Many other professionals from all over the country who have attended institutes and offered constructive criticism have enabled the continual improvement of LETRS and related materials. We hope you see your influence on all of the second edition modules.

We are grateful for the competent support of the Sopris West editorial and production staff, including Holly Bell, Jeff Dieffenbach, Michelle LaBorde, Rob Carson, Karen Butler, Sherri Rowe, Geoff Horsfall, Jill Stanko, and Kay Power. Special thanks are due to Toni Backstrom, who manages the LETRS program with enthusiasm, competence, and flare, and to Steve Mitchell, the publisher of LETRS.

About the Authors

Louisa C. Moats, Ed.D., is a nationally recognized authority on reading instruction, how children learn to read, why many people have trouble reading, and treatment of reading problems. Louisa has been a neuropsychology technician, teacher, graduate school instructor, licensed psychologist, researcher, conference speaker, and author. She spent 15 years in private practice in Vermont, specializing in evaluation of and consultation with individuals of all ages who experienced difficulty with reading, spelling, writing, and oral language. After advising the California Reading Initiative for one year, Louisa was site director of the NICHD Early Interventions Project in Washington, D.C., a four-year project that included daily work with inner-city teachers and children. Recently, she has devoted herself to the improvement of teacher training and professional development.

Louisa earned her bachelor's degree at Wellesley College, her master's degree at Peabody College of Vanderbilt, and her doctorate in reading and human development from the Harvard Graduate School of Education. She was licensed to teach in three states before undertaking her doctoral work. In addition to LETRS®, Louisa has authored and coauthored books including *Speech to Print: Language Essentials for Teachers*; *Spelling: Development, Disability, and Instruction*; *Straight Talk About Reading* (with Susan Hall), *Parenting a Struggling Reader* (with Susan Hall), and *Basic Facts About Dyslexia and Other Reading Problems* (with Karen Dakin). Instructional materials include *Spellography* (with Bruce Rosow) and *Spelling by Pattern* (with Ellen Javernick and Betty Hooper).

Louisa's many journal articles, book chapters, and policy papers include the American Federation of Teachers' *Teaching Reading Is Rocket Science*, the Learning First Alliance's *Every Child Reading: A Professional Development Guide*, and Reading First's *Blueprint for Professional Development*.

Marcia Davidson, Ph.D., is a faculty member in the College of Education at the University of Utah. She teaches courses on language and literacy, interventions for reading difficulties, assessment, and Response to Intervention (RtI). Marcia is a national LETRS trainer and, as a nationally certified school psychologist, has worked with children from preschool through age 21 and families in public schools for 15 years. She earned her Ph.D. in special education at the University of Washington and has been a faculty member in departments of special education and elementary education. Marcia was a senior research associate at RMC Research Corporation for several years and provided technical assistance to states in the implementation of Reading First. Her research interests are in the areas of reading fluency, teacher knowledge and behaviors, early intervention, and assessment. Marcia has published articles and book chapters on curriculum-based measures, assessment, and early literacy.

Contents

Chapter 3 Improving Fluency in Each Tier of Instruction

Chapter 4 **The Measurement of Reading Fluency**

Introduction to LETRS®

LETRS® (*Language Essentials for Teachers of Reading and Spelling*) is professional development for educators who are responsible for improving K–12 instruction in reading, writing, and spelling. The content of LETRS is delivered in a series of 12 core modules in book format. Each module in the series focuses on one topic, with the topics aligned to be delivered in sequential training. Thus, one book for use in the course of training—and later as a professional reference—is provided for each module. Each module is typically delivered in a one- to two-day presentation by a national, regional, or local district trainer who has met the LETRS trainer certification guidelines developed by Dr. Moats and her colleagues.

> **module [mŏjūl] n.**
> a self-contained component of a whole that is used in conjunction with, and has a well-defined connection to, the other components

LETRS modules are used for both in-service training and for undergraduate and graduate courses in reading and literacy. They can also be resources for any educator charged with improving the language skills of students. LETRS is designed so that participants will understand:

1. *How* children learn to read and *why* some children have difficulty with this aspect of literacy;
2. *What* must be taught during reading and spelling lessons and *how to teach* most effectively;
3. *Why* all components of reading instruction are necessary and *how* they are related;
4. *How to interpret* individual differences in student achievement; and
5. *How to explain* the form and structure of English.

LETRS modules are designed to be delivered in sequence, but flexible sequencing is possible. In sequence, the modules build on overview concepts and introductory content, and then on phonology, phoneme awareness, and the writing system (orthography) of English (Modules 1–3). Next, the modules progress to topics in vocabulary, fluency, and comprehension instruction (Modules 4–6). Later modules (7–9) target reading instruction for the primary grades and include a module on assessment for prevention and early intervention. The final series (Modules 10–12), designed for educators who work with students at grade 3 and above, address advanced phonics and word study, comprehension and study skills in content-area reading, and assessment.

A presenter CD-ROM (developed by Dr. Carol Tolman) accompanies each LETRS module, providing a PowerPoint® presentation that supports, extends, and elaborates module content. The presentation slides are designed to be used by professional development personnel, higher education faculty, consultants, reading specialists, and coaches who have a strong background in the concepts and who have been trained to deliver LETRS modules.

LETRS is not a reading instruction program, and LETRS modules do not substitute for program-specific training. Rather, LETRS complements and supports the implementation of programs aligned with scientifically based reading research (SBRR). A complete approach to improving reading instruction must include: (a) selection and use of core and supplemental instructional materials; (b) professional development on how to use the materials; (c) professional development that leads to broader understandings; (d) classroom coaching and in-school supports; (e) an assessment program for data-based problem-solving; and (f) strong leadership. A comprehensive, systemic approach with these elements will support a Response to Intervention (RtI) initiative.

We recommend that teachers who have had little experience with or exposure to the science of reading and research-based practices begin with LETRS *Foundations* (Glaser & Moats, 2008). *Foundations* is a stepping stone into the regular LETRS modules. Other related resources have been developed to support LETRS professional development, including:

- LETRS Interactive CD-ROMs for Modules 2, 3, 4, 7, and 8 (developed with a grant from the Small Business Innovation Research [SBIR] program of the National Institute of Child Health and Human Development [NICHD]), which provide additional content and skill practice for topics often considered challenging to implement and teach in the classroom.
- *ParaReading: A Training Guide for Tutors* (Glaser, 2005)
- *The Reading Coach: A How-To Manual for Success* (Hasbrouck & Denton, 2005)
- *Teaching English Language Learners: A Supplementary* LETRS® *Module* (Arguelles & Baker, in press)
- *Early Childhood* LETRS (Hart Paulson, in press)
- *Teaching Reading Essentials* (Moats & Farrell, 2007), a series of video modeling used extensively by LETRS trainers throughout the delivery of training.

The chart on the next page represents a fundamental idea in LETRS—that language systems underlie reading and writing, and students' difficulties with reading and writing are most effectively addressed if the structures and functions of language are taught to them directly. We ask teachers to learn the terminology of language systems and to recognize that language is an important common denominator that links reading with writing, speaking, and listening comprehension.

Content of LETRS Modules Within the Language-Literacy Connection

Components of Comprehensive Reading Instruction	Organization of Language						
	Phonology	Morphology	Orthography	Semantics	Syntax	Discourse and Pragmatics	Etymology
Phonological Awareness	2	2					
Phonics, Spelling, and Word Study	3, 7	3, 7, 10	3, 7, 10				3, 10
Fluency	5	5	5	5	5	5	
Vocabulary	4	4	4	4	4		4
Text Comprehension		6		6	6	6, 11	
Written Expression			9, 11	9, 11	9, 11	9, 11	
Assessment	8, 12	8, 12	8, 12	8, 12	8, 12	8, 12	

Note: Numbers represent individual modules in the LETRS series.

Overview of Module 5

Module 5 defines reading fluency and explains the close relationship between oral reading fluency and reading comprehension. Building on models of reading acquisition introduced in previous LETRS modules, it explains and illustrates why and how fluency in component reading skills leads to fluent reading of text. Many research-based techniques for building fluency at each tier of instruction (i.e., classroom, small-group, intensive intervention) are demonstrated and practiced. This module concludes with a chapter on progress monitoring with curriculum-based fluency measures.

Chapter 1

The Importance of Fluency in Learning to Read

Learner Objectives for Chapter 1
- Define the term *reading fluency*.
- Interpret national and international data on reading fluency and reading proficiency.
- Participate in an experiment with oral reading fluency.

Warm-Up: World Bank Video
- Watch a video produced by the World Bank on the use of reading fluency as a key indicator of overall reading proficiency and consider the following questions:

1. Why do you think that 60 words correct per minute (WCPM) was the criterion chosen to represent a minimal level of fluency for second-grade children in Peru?

   Average on how well they could comprehend what was read.
   1 word/ second

   Sight words word/second

2. Why were the children asked to answer questions about what they read?

   So you could know if they understood what they read

3. What did you learn about the children who were learning to read fluently in two languages?

Defining "Reading Fluency"

Before reading this chapter, take a minute to write your own definition of *reading fluency*:

reading accurate, very smooth, not choppy, making sense of your reading passages, reading with expression

The term *reading fluency* has been defined in different ways by various experts. The term may be used to refer to the natural vocal cadence and smooth phrasing of a person who is reading aloud with comprehension. The term may also refer to an oral reading fluency (ORF) measure or statistic: rate and accuracy in oral reading. The concept is also invoked to describe silent-reading fluency rates in proficient readers, distinguishing between those who read at typical rates and those who speed-read. Because different definitions of reading fluency exist, we must establish a working definition of the term to anchor our work in this module. With a clear definition, we will have an easier time understanding:

- why fluency is a concern in reading development;
- how to identify fluency-based problems in reading; and
- how to address the problems in instruction.

Here is a good definition of fluency, synthesized from the Report of the National Reading Panel (National Institute of Child Health and Human Development [NICHD], 2000) and other sources (Pikulski & Chard, 2005):

> Reading fluency refers to efficient, effective word recognition skills that permit a reader to construct the meaning of text. Fluency is manifested in accurate, rapid, expressive oral reading and is applied during, and makes possible, silent reading comprehension.

Another, similar definition (Hudson, Mercer, & Lane, 2000) that encapsulates this idea is:

> Fluency is accurate reading at a minimal rate with appropriate prosodic features (expression) and deep understanding.

In brief, our goal is *reading fluency that is sufficient to support comprehension*. What are the key ideas in these definitions? Let's take them one at a time.

1. **Automaticity in word recognition**. Efficient word recognition occurs without conscious effort, at an automatic level. Word recognition is automatic when the process takes very few of the attention resources available to the brain at any one time (Samuels, 1997). The brain has only a limited amount of "desk space" or attention capacity. Reading is no different than most complex behaviors mastered by humans. Almost any learned activity requires a set of underlying subskills that must be learned to an automatic level so that attention is devoted to problem-solving, synthesis of ideas, self-monitoring, or other types of reasoning. Great

basketball coaches ask their players to practice and master ball handling, footwork, court coverage, and other skills until they can use them instantly in the service of complex plays. Pianists learn finger positions, keys, scales, chords, and other aspects of musicianship before and during their interpretive musical performances. Readers must rapidly recognize printed words, spacing, word meanings, and punctuation conventions to comprehend written text.

fluency d
accuracy
important

2. **Accurate word recognition**. It is not only speed that matters, but accuracy as well. Speed is not possible without accuracy. Every time a reader misreads a word, meaning may be lost or eroded. If students cannot recognize words accurately, they will almost always be slow, and they will almost always have difficulty with comprehension.

3. **Prosody, or expression**. We can tell by listening to a person reading aloud whether they are fluent or not. A person who reads fluently sounds as if they understand what they are reading, and helps the listener understand as well. The fluent reader supplies phrasing and emphasis while reading aloud. Phrasing and emphasis are manifestations of comprehension, and comprehension may occur as a consequence of fast, accurate word-reading.

4. **Sufficient to permit comprehension**. Importantly, this criterion for fluency suggests that there is a threshold of accuracy and speed that is sufficient to focus on the meanings of the text. This criterion states that the reader should reach a baseline, or benchmark, level of automatic word-reading that will allow him to focus on meanings.

Automaticity in Word Recognition

* Capacity for performance without conscious attention.
* All complex behaviors require automaticity in underlying skills!

prosody \prŏ-sə-dē\ *n*

inflected form(s):
— *plural* **pros·o·dies**
etymology:
— Middle English, from Latin *prosodia*, accent of a syllable, from Greek *prosōidia*, song sung to instrumental music, accent, from *pros* in addition to + *ōidē* song.
date: 15th century

1. the study of versification; *esp*: the systematic study of metrical structure
2. a particular system, theory, or style of versification
3. **the rhythmic and intonational aspect of language**

Note that *not one* definition embraces the idea that faster reading is necessarily better reading, beyond a critical threshold. More will be said about each aspect of fluency, and the research underlying these concepts, as we progress through this module.

An International Perspective on Reading Fluency

In the video clip you viewed, children in Peru are being asked to read aloud to determine whether they can read fluently in Spanish. Peru has established a national standard for reading fluency for second-grade children and uses this metric as a simple, easy-to-use estimate of how well children can read and how successful their instruction in reading has been. Peru's case is just one example of an international trend to employ fluency as a metric for reading proficiency.

The international effort to employ fluency as a metric in evaluating the success of literacy efforts in developing countries is a combination of efforts from psychologists and other experts at the World Bank and Research Triangle Institute (RTI)-International in North Carolina.

In 2006, Matthew Jukes and colleagues (Jukes, Vagh, & Kim, 2006) reviewed the role of reading assessments in developing countries for the World Bank. Their paper described the research on early reading skills and assessments and the devastating consequences for young children who are identified as poor readers at an early age (Jukes et al., p. 3):

> This is a finding of great concern given the low academic achievement levels reported for children in early grades in poor, developing societies. This underscores the importance of early literacy instruction and indicates that there is an overwhelming need to monitor early literacy development and the attainment of early reading goals via appropriate reading assessments in order to effectively inform the design of standard and/or intervention programs.

Jukes et al. concluded, as other researchers (Wolf & Katzir-Cohen (2001) have, "that reading fluency involves every process and subskill involved in reading (p. 220)." Therefore, reading fluency measures—simple and inexpensive—were deemed reliable and valid indicators that could be used by governments interested in tracking reading achievement and reading progress in their student populations. Jukes et al. recommended that a multi-country pilot study be conducted using fluency measures, including comprehension questions, as the framework for assessing reading internationally.

There are now pilot data from several developing countries that have begun to develop what is now referred to as Early Grade Reading Assessments (EGRA). To date, more than 12 developing countries—Nicaragua, Senegal, Gambia, and Romania, among others—are engaged in screening young children with a battery of reading assessments that focus on rate and accuracy, often in two languages. The projects also include working with teachers in the development of effective reading interventions. The effort has involved educators and policymakers at the national and local levels in order that these practices are grounded in local communities in each country.

A Study of Reading Fluency in the United States

In both 1992 and 2002, studies of reading fluency in fourth-graders were undertaken in association with the National Assessment of Educational Progress (NAEP; 1992, 2002). This biannual assessment of academic skills is the only national assessment that allows us to compare reading achievement across 40 or more participating states.

Researchers identified a subsample of students randomly selected from the sample of fourth-graders who took the NAEP reading assessment (National Center for Education Statistics [NCES], 2002). The selected students represented a range of abilities, from low- to high-level reading performance. The connection between silent passage-reading comprehension (with a multiple-choice question format) and oral reading fluency rates is clearly seen in *Figure 1.1*.

[handwritten: Silent passage – reading comprehension with multiple choice format]

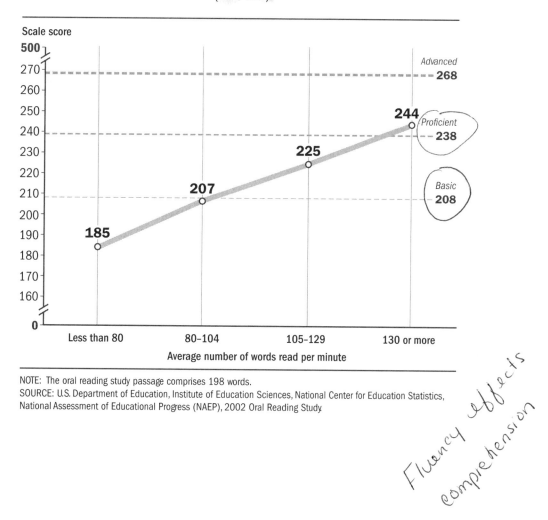

Figure 1.1 Reading Achievement and Reading Rate
(NAEP, 2002)

NOTE: The oral reading study passage comprises 198 words.
SOURCE: U.S. Department of Education, Institute of Education Sciences, National Center for Education Statistics, National Assessment of Educational Progress (NAEP), 2002 Oral Reading Study.

[handwritten: Fluency effects comprehension]

Figure 1.1 shows that rate and accuracy in oral reading fluency are closely related to overall reading skill, as measured in silent-reading comprehension. Higher fluency scores were associated with higher average reading scores. Reading rate was positively related to reading comprehension. Although one cannot assume a simple causal relationship between fluent oral reading and reading comprehension, " … it would seem likely that the more competent readers, with larger reading vocabularies, well-developed word-reading skills, and an ability to comprehend grade-appropriate texts, could read through a text at a faster rate than students with less skill in these areas." (NAEP, 2002, p. 37)

A few key findings from the 2002 NAEP study of oral reading were as follows:

- Approximately 75 percent of the fourth-grade students in the NAEP sample read the passage with at least 95 percent accuracy when reading aloud.

- The 19 percent of students who scored at the "basic" level read with 90–94 percent accuracy on average during oral reading.

- The 6 percent of students who read with less than 90 percent accuracy scored 20 points, on average, below the "basic" level cut-score. Low reading rates were clearly associated with poor overall reading skills.

- When reading rate was defined as *words per minute* for the entire length of the excerpt, the results were quite different than those obtained when defining reading rate as the *words read in the first minute of reading*:
  - Rate defined as reading for the first minute: 56 percent read 130 or more words.
  - Rate defined as words per minute over the entire length of the passage: 27 percent read at least 130 words per minute.

Educators must be very cautious in how they define reading rate and accuracy because the measures yield quite different results! Longer, sustained oral reading typically produces lower reading rates than one-minute timed samples.

The type and frequency of errors in fourth-graders' oral reading varied by reading proficiency levels (*Figure 1.2*). The less well that students read, the more likely their oral reading errors reflected miscomprehension of the passage. The better that students read, the more likely their errors preserved the meaning of the passage.

These findings provide concrete evidence for the close relationship between reading comprehension, reading fluency, and word-reading accuracy. Before we delve into the implications of these data, let's document our own fluency rates in *Exercise 1.1*.

Figure 1.2 Meaning-Change Errors and Reading Fluency
(NAEP data, 2002)

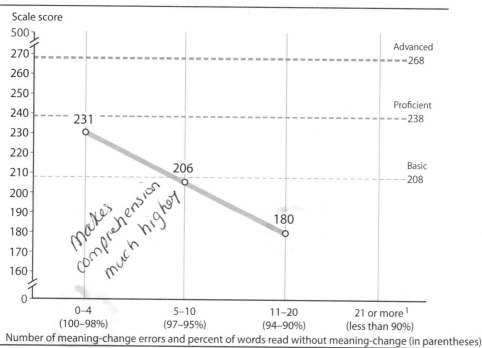

Scale score

Number of meaning-change errors and percent of words read without meaning-change (in parentheses)

[1] Sample size was insufficient to permit a reliable estimate for students with 21 or more errors that resulted in a change of meaning.

SOURCE: U.S. Department of Education, Institute of Education Sciences, National Center for Education Statistics, National Assessment of Educational Progress (NAEP), 2002 Oral Reading Study.

Exercise 1.1 | An Experiment in Oral Reading Fluency

- Partner up. Be sure you have a timer.

- Partner 1 keeps time while monitoring Partner 2's oral reading accuracy and rate of the first exercise passage. Partner 2 will read for one minute at a comfortable, natural pace, with expression. (Pay attention to what you are reading, because you may be asked to retell the main events.)

- After one minute, Partner 2 stops reading and Partner 1 calculates the number of words correct per minute (WCPM) read by Partner 2.

- Partner 2 then reads the second passage in this exercise for one minute. Partner 1 calculates Partner 2's WCPM of the second passage.

- Then partners reverse roles, with Partner 1 reading and Partner 2 calculating Partner 1's WCPM of both exercise passages.

- After both partners have read both passages and calculated each other's WCPMs, discuss why your reading rates differed on the two passages.

- As a class, calculate the average oral reading rate.

(continued)

Exercise 1.1   (continued)

Passage 1: From *Alice's Adventures in Wonderland,* by Lewis Carroll (1866)

Chapter 1: "Down the Rabbit Hole"

Alice was beginning to get very tired of sitting by her sister on the bank,	15
and of having nothing to do: once or twice she had peeped into the book her	31
sister was reading, but it had no pictures or conversations in it, "and what is the	47
use of a book," thought Alice, "without pictures or conversations?"	57
So she was considering in her own mind, (as well as she could, for the hot	73
day made her feel very sleepy and stupid), whether the pleasure of making a	87
daisy-chain would be worth the trouble of getting up and picking the daisies,	100
when suddenly a white rabbit with pink eyes ran close by her.	112
There was nothing so *very* remarkable in that; nor did Alice think it so very	127
much out of the way to hear the Rabbit say to itself, "Oh dear! Oh dear! I	144
shall be too late!" (when she thought it over afterwards, it occurred to her that	159
she ought to have wondered at this, but at the time it all seemed quite natural);	175
but when the Rabbit actually *took a watch out of its waistcoat-pocket,* and looked	189
at it, and then hurried on, Alice started to her feet, for it flashed across her	206
mind that she had never before seen a rabbit with either a waistcoat-pocket or	220
a watch to take out of it, and, burning with curiosity, she ran across the field	236
after it, and was just in time to see it pop down a large rabbit-hole under the	253
hedge. In another moment down went Alice after it, never once considering	265
how in the world she was to get out again.	275
The rabbit-hole went straight on like a tunnel for some way, and then	288
dipped suddenly down, so suddenly that Alice had not a moment to think	301
about stopping herself before she found herself falling down what seemed to	313
be a very deep well.	318
Either the well was very deep, or she fell very slowly, for she had plenty of	334
time as she went down to look about her, and to wonder what was going to	350
happen next. First, she tried to look down and make out what she was coming	365
to, but it was too dark to see anything: then she looked at the sides of the well,	383
and noticed that they were filled with cupboards and bookshelves: here and	395
there she saw maps and pictures hung upon pegs. She took down a jar from	410
one of the shelves she passed; it was labeled "ORANGE MARMALADE"	421
but to her great disappointment it was empty: she did not like to drop the jar	437
for fear of killing somebody underneath, so managed to put it into one of the	452
cupboards as she fell past it.	458

(continued)

Exercise 1.1 (continued)

"Well!" thought Alice to herself, "after such a fall as this, I shall think nothing   473
of tumbling down stairs! How brave they'll all think me at home! Why, I   487
wouldn't say anything about it, even if I fell off the top of the house!" (Which   503
was very likely true.)   507

Down, down, down. Would the fall never come to an end? "I wonder   520
how many miles I've fallen by this time?" she said aloud. "I must be getting   535
somewhere near the center of the earth. Let me see: that would be four   549
thousand miles down, I think" (for, you see, Alice had learnt several things   563
of this sort in her lessons in the school-room, and though this was not a *very*   578
good opportunity for showing off her knowledge, as there was no one to   591
listen to her, still it was good practice to say it over) "yes—that's about the   607
right distance—but then I wonder what Latitude or Longitude I've got to?"   620
(Alice had not the slightest idea what Latitude was, or Longitude either, but   633
she thought they were nice grand words to say.)   642

Passage 2: From *Scientific Studies of Reading* (Graham, Harris, Fink, & MacArthur, 2001)

To analyze the underlying factor structure of the 16-item Teacher Efficacy   11
Scale for Writing, the responses of the participating primary grade teachers   22
were analyzed through exploratory factor analysis. Initially, an unconstrained   31
principal factor analysis was used to generate the factor matrix with squared   43
multiple correlations as initial communality estimates. Items that exhibited   52
factor structure loadings of .40 or greater were used to define a factor.   65

Prior to rotation, the unconstrained principal factor analysis produced four   75
factors with eigenvalues greater than 1.0. The four factors accounted for 60%   87
of the total test variance. Their respective eigenvalues were 4.7, 2.57, 1.31,   99
and 1.09. Based on a scree plot of the eigenvalues and theoretical concurrence   112
with models of teacher efficacy, a two-factor solution was rotated by using the   125
varimax solution.   127

Results for the forced two-factor solution revealed that the varimax rotation   138
accounted for 38% of the total test score variance. As can be seen in Table   153
2, 10 of the 16 rotated items loaded at .40 or greater on the first factor. This   170
factor appeared to reflect teachers' beliefs about their ability to teach writing   182
and affect change in their students. Consistent with prior research, we labeled   194
this factor personal teaching efficacy. The other six rotated items loaded at .40   207
or greater on the second factor.   213

(continued)

Exercise 1.1   (continued)

- Was there a difference in your reading speed or comprehension between the two passages?
- Was there a difference in your level of enjoyment?
- What is the relationship between reading fluency, type of text, and ability to comprehend?

_____

_____

Quick Write: Questions About Fluency?

- Write three questions that you hope to have answered by the completion of this module.

  1. _____

     _____

  2. _____

     _____

  3. _____

     _____

- Share your questions with a partner.
- Choose one question you are the most interested in having answered, and write it on a self-stick note. Share your question with the group or post it for the group to read.

How Do Children Become Fluent Readers?

Learner Objectives for Chapter 2
- Learn the importance of automaticity and fluency for reading connected text.
- Review the role of fluency in reading development.
- Explore tasks used for building fluency in component skills of reading.

Warm-Up: Review Fluency and the Four-Part Processing Model for Word Recognition

- Draw the Four-Part Processing model of word recognition from memory, if you can. (If you are unfamiliar with this model, consult LETRS Module 1, *Figure 3.4*, on page 33.)

- Explain how fluent word recognition is represented in this model.

_____

_____

Fluency: A Consequence of Proficiency in Reading Subskills

Reading fluency is both a cause and a consequence of one's reading experience and reading habits. Research indicates that good readers, who recognize words instantly and use phonic decoding skills easily and accurately, read much more than poor readers do right from the beginning of their school years (Cunningham & Stanovich, 1991, 1998; Torgesen et al., 2001). Good readers practice reading early and often; thus, they are exposed to printed words far more than children who read very little. Good readers who begin school with an aptitude for and/or knowledge of sounds, letters, and words get significantly more print exposure from the first part of first grade because they enjoy the activity of reading.

In contrast, poor readers, who struggle with word recognition and/or comprehension, tend to avoid reading because it demands attention, persistence, and effort. Consequently, they are exposed to far fewer words, get less practice, and remain uncomfortable with a task that is often frustrating and unrewarding. These readers almost always fail to develop automaticity in the subskills necessary for reading to be enjoyable, so they practice far less than they should. This cycle must be broken if poor readers are to become proficient readers.

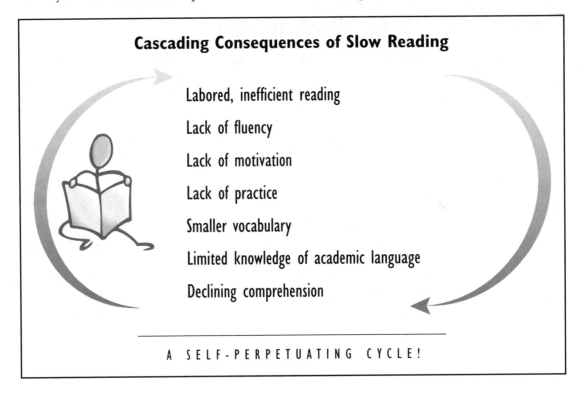

Cascading Consequences of Slow Reading

Labored, inefficient reading

Lack of fluency

Lack of motivation

Lack of practice

Smaller vocabulary

Limited knowledge of academic language

Declining comprehension

A S E L F - P E R P E T U A T I N G   C Y C L E !

If we were to focus only on the surface symptom of a reading problem—slow oral reading—we could easily miss the underlying causes and conclude that all we need to do is give children more reading practice. However, considerable research support exists for systematically addressing the subskills that lead to fluent oral reading. Ehri's developmental framework (Ehri, 1996, 2004; Ehri & Snowling, 2004) for understanding printed word recognition, introduced in Module 1, provides a reliable reference point for conceptualizing the building blocks that must be in place.

Ehri's Model of Word Recognition

The phases of word recognition described in *Figure 2.1* and *Table 2.1* characterize students of varying levels of proficiency in basic reading skill. The development of word recognition and spelling include prealphabetic, early alphabetic, later alphabetic, and consolidated alphabetic phases, in which students become aware of speech sounds and connect them to print. Some students move through these phases quite effortlessly, or "naturally," but others move through them much more slowly and with much more effort.

Figure 2.1   Ehri's Phases of Word-Reading Development

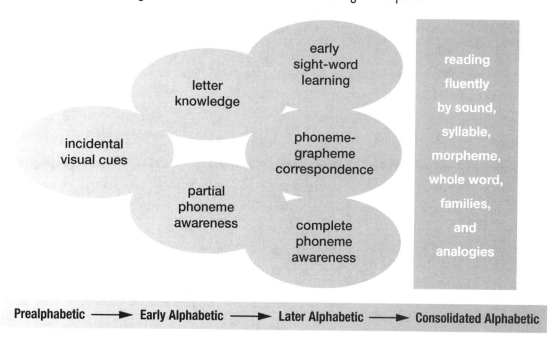

Table 2.1   Ehri's Phases of Reading and Spelling Development
(based on Ehri & Snowling, 2004)

	Prealphabetic phase	Early Alphabetic phase	Later Alphabetic phase	Consolidated Alphabetic phase
How a child reads familiar words	Rote learning of incidental visual features of a word; no letter-sound awareness	Partial use of letter-sound correspondence; initial sound and salient consonants	Pronunciation of whole words on the basis of complete phoneme-grapheme mapping	Reads variously by phonemes, syllabic units, morpheme units, and whole words

(continued)

	Prealphabetic phase	Early Alphabetic phase	Later Alphabetic phase	Consolidated Alphabetic phase
How a child reads unfamiliar words	Guessing is constrained by context or memory of text	Constrained by context; gets first sound and guesses	Full use of phoneme-grapheme correspondence; blends all sounds left to right; begins to use analogy to known patterns	Sequential and hierarchical decoding; notices familiar parts first, reads by analogy to similar known words
Other indicators	Dependent on context; few words; errors and confusions; cannot read text	Similar-appearing words are confused	Rapid, unitized reading of whole familiar words is increasing	Remembers multisyllabic words; analogizes easily, associates word structure with meaning
Spelling	Strings letters together, assigns meaning without representing sounds in words	Represents a few salient sounds, such as beginning and ending consonants; fills in other letters randomly; knows some letter names for sounds	Phonetically accurate; beginning to incorporate conventional letter sequences and patterns; sight-word knowledge is increasing	Word knowledge includes language of origin; morphemes; syntactic role; ending rules; prefix, suffix, and root forms

The component subskills in Ehri's framework (Ehri, 1996, 2004; Ehri & Snowling, 2004) develop sequentially and in parallel. (See also Vellutino, Tunmer, Jaccard, & Chen, 2007, for a thorough analysis of the components of reading and how they develop over time.) For example, a child in the early alphabetic phase may be starting to learn a few words "by sight" and may have noticed some of the patterns of print. Importantly, however, the model allows us to identify and measure the subskills that enable a student to be accurate and fluent in word recognition. *Figure 2.2*, Scarborough's "rope" model, depicts how those subskills relate to one another as a child learns to read and spell words.

Figure 2.2 The Path to Fluent Reading for Meaning
(Scarborough, 2001)

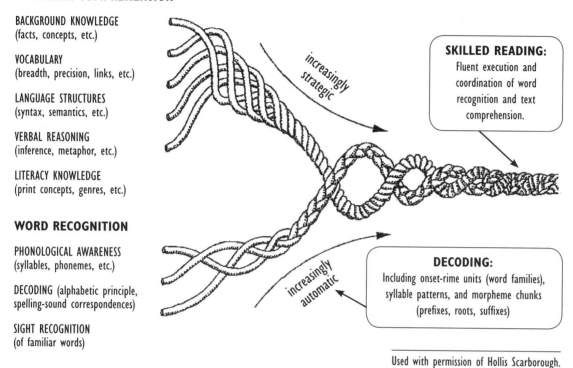

Used with permission of Hollis Scarborough.

The subskills identified in *Figure 2.2* are gradually automatized as fluent reading is learned. These subskills include recognition of letters, speech sounds, letter-sound correspondences, rime chunks, syllable patterns, morphemes, and whole words. In addition, as the model shows, the more quickly a student associates a meaning to a printed word, the more rapidly the student recognizes the word. Thus, vocabulary and language comprehension will also affect reading fluency. If a student hesitates about which sound a grapheme represents, or can't recognize the meaning of an intended word, she will be slowed down and may not be able to hold the meaning of the whole sentence or passage in mind.

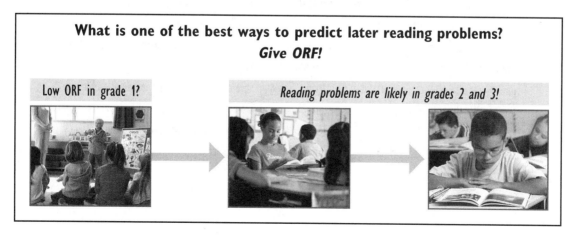

Many researchers have documented that oral reading fluency (ORF) is an excellent early predictor of later reading difficulties, no matter what the background of the student (Fuchs, Fuchs, Hosp, & Jenkins, 2001; Good, Simmons, & Kame'enui, 2001; Kame'enui & Simmons, 2001; Speece & Ritchey, 2005). Correlations between ORF in first grade and silent-reading comprehension in third grade are as high as .91 (Fuchs et al., 2001). Speece and Ritchey recently examined whether ORF was an early predictor of later reading difficulties. By the end of first grade, children who were identified as "at risk" at the beginning of first grade read less than half the words and were progressing at about half the rate of their typically achieving peers. The authors found that word-level skills (represented by ORF) in first grade were powerful predictors of achievement in second grade. Further, children who made better progress in first grade performed better on the high-stakes outcome measure, regardless of their starting point. Speece and Ritchey's study points to the importance of both rate of progress and level of performance as children acquire early reading skills. It also confirms that the reading skills children bring to the classroom—even in first grade—will predict where they are in reading way down the road, unless intervention is intensive and effective for those at risk.

Importantly, Speece and Ritchey (2005; see abstract, following) documented that reading fluency problems are evident in the early stages of reading development, at the time students are acquiring phonic word-attack skills. Thus, the development of reading fluency may need to be viewed as a *concomitant* process in the earliest stages of learning to read words rather than merely a stage of development between decoding and comprehension, as Chall (1996) originally proposed. The facility with which children are able to read as early as the middle of first grade has an impact on second-grade performance, and possibly beyond. Early reading instruction may need to target not only word recognition but also *fluent* word recognition and fluent execution of the subskills that contribute to word reading (Chall, p. 397).

(Speece & Ritchey, 2005)

Abstract: The purpose of this study was to examine the development of oral reading fluency in a sample of first-grade children. Using growth curve analysis, models of growth were identified for a combined sample of at-risk (AR) and not-at-risk (NAR) children, and predictors of growth were identified for the longitudinal AR sample in first and second grade. Large and serious differences in reading fluency growth between the AR and NAR samples were apparent early, replicating other reports. Theories of sight-word learning and reading fluency were supported, in that letter-sound fluency was a uniquely significant predictor of first-grade reading fluency. The effects of phonological awareness and rapid automatized naming were mediated by the other variables in the model. Growth in first-grade oral reading fluency accounted for the most unique variance in second-grade growth and end-of-year performance. The results suggest that word reading fluency should be regarded as developing concomitantly with early word recognition rather than as a later-developing skill.

It is also true that some students with vocabulary and oral language comprehension weaknesses—especially ELLs—may have adequate or average word-recognition skills and may be at benchmark in ORF but may not have the language comprehension abilities to pass high-stakes reading comprehension tests. For example, the state of Florida collects both reading fluency data and silent-reading comprehension data from its students. Some students who meet ORF benchmarks do not pass the end-of-year, silent-passage reading test given in Florida (Tihen, 2007). The correlations between these two forms of assessment are high, but not perfect, especially at grade 5 and beyond.

What Contributes to Automaticity?

What do we mean when we say that we want readers to recognize most words automatically? Let's take a closer look at the factors involved. Stanovich (1990) differentiated three aspects of automaticity in word recognition: (a) rapid speed of recognition; (b) reduced need for attention; and (c) the "obligatory" aspect of word recognition (i.e., the "Stroop effect"): that is, when we see a word we recognize, we access its meaning automatically (Stroop, 1935). We cannot keep our minds from accessing the meaning of the word once we have learned it. The "obligatory" aspect of word recognition seems to develop fairly quickly, while the speed of word recognition and the reduced need for attention develop more slowly.

Exercise 2.1   Experience the "Stroop Effect"

- Look at the words on the presenter's slide.

- Name the <u>colors</u> (not the words!) as quickly as you can.

- Compare the time it took you to name the colors (of the print itself) with the time it took to read the words.

RED	GREEN	BLUE	YELLOW	PINK
ORANGE	BLUE	GREEN	BLUE	WHITE
GREEN	YELLOW	ORANGE	BLUE	WHITE
BROWN	RED	BLUE	YELLOW	GREEN
PINK	YELLOW	GREEN	BLUE	RED

1. Was it difficult to name the colors quickly without attending to the words? Why is it easier to read the words than name the colors?

_____

_____

2. How does automatic word-reading affect fluency?

_____

_____

S. Jay Samuels (1997) and his colleagues (Samuels & Flor, 1997; see abstract, following) have researched the relationships among automaticity, fluency, and comprehension since the 1970s. They argue that automaticity of the kind just demonstrated is purposeful because it enhances the likelihood that information accessed through reading will be stored in long-term memory. Reading skills that are merely accurate may not be serviceable. Consider, for example, that you may have learned how to hold and swing a golf club, but until you can count on the consistent and automatic execution of that swing, you will have trouble implementing your game plan.

(Samuels & Flor, 1997)

Abstract: Automaticity refers to the ability to perform complex skills with minimal attention and conscious effort. Automaticity is essential for higher-order thinking, such as skilled reading and writing, because important sub-skills must be performed accurately, quickly, and effortlessly. If reading sub-skills are performed automatically, then higher-order aspects of the task, such as comprehension or meta-cognitive functions, can be performed effectively at the same time. How do students become automatic at these sub-skills? What are the indicators that can be used to determine whether a student is automatic? What are the psychological mechanisms that allow one to perform complex skills automatically? These questions are addressed in this article.

Automaticity in processing print is a hallmark of fluent reading. On the other hand, automaticity without focus or purpose is of little use. Have you ever planned a short trip to a unique destination only to find that your mind wandered to a movie you recently saw and, before you knew it, you automatically took the route to work instead of to your new destination? Why? You navigated a very familiar route without conscious attention, but you forgot to think about where you were going. Automaticity allows us to ponder our actions, but we can be so automatic that we miss the opportunity to monitor what we are doing—whether it is reading or driving. When we read, monitoring and attending to the meaning of what we are reading must accompany the automatic reading of words in order to maximize the benefit of that skill.

Teaching Tip
- Text-reading fluency assessment and instruction should *always* have a comprehension component!

may not be a test

Developing Fluency in the Component Skills of Reading

Pikulski and Chard (2005) make a strong case for explicit instruction of component skills to help students attain fluent reading. Ehri's (1996, 2004) phases of word recognition provide the conceptual foundation for the fluency-building teaching strategies elaborated in this chapter. These practices include those advocated by Pikulski and Chard as well as those advocated by Berninger and Richards (2002), Meyer and Felton (1999), and Wolf (2003) that are found in effective intervention programs. In addition, Beck and Clement (1991) demonstrated with regular classroom, intermediate students that brief remedial sessions to build fluent performance of component academic skills had a large, positive influence on overall reading and language arts achievement.

As students acquire reading skills, they must be accurate and reasonably fluent with the parallel strands depicted in Scarborough's (2001) "rope" model (refer back to *Figure 2.2*) in order to move through Ehri's (1996, 2004) phases. To conceptualize the progression of skills that must be automatic to be useful, let's look again at the hourglass figure originally introduced in Modules 2 and 3:

Figure 2.3 The Hourglass Progression, Phonology to Orthography
(Contributed by Carol Tolman, used with permission)

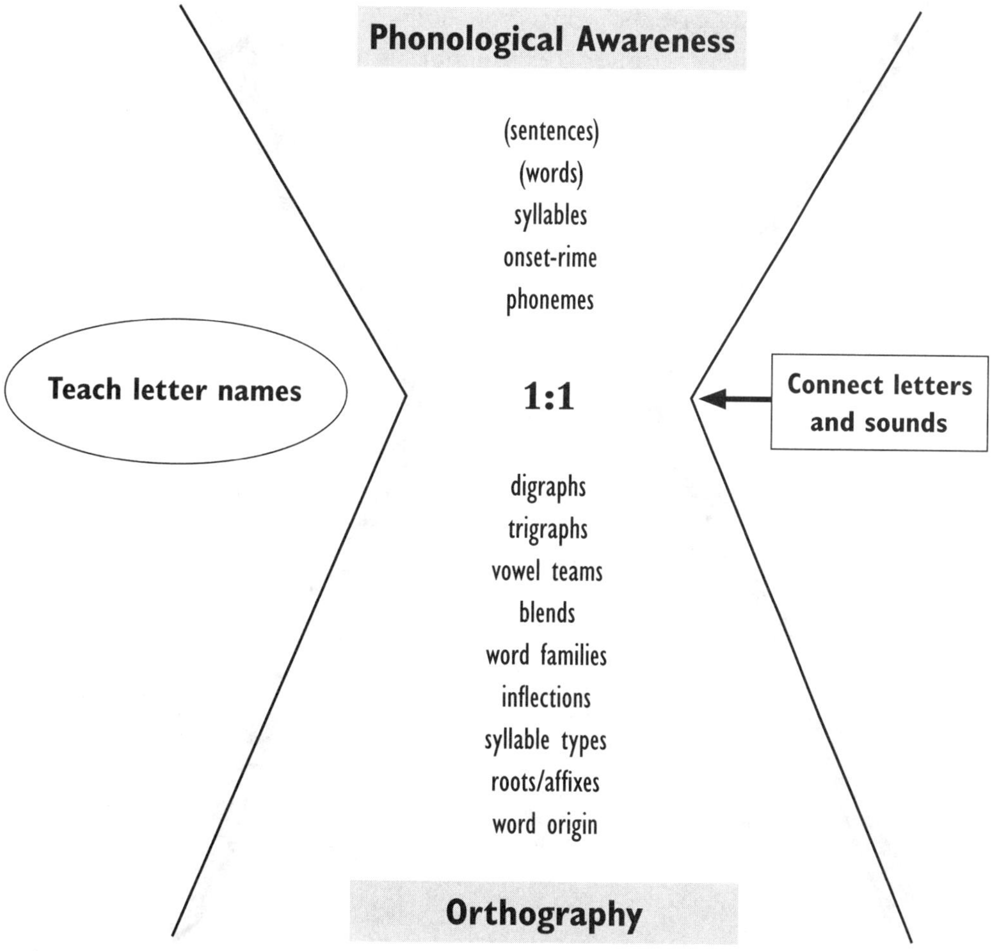

Phonological Awareness

(sentences)
(words)
syllables
onset-rime
phonemes

Teach letter names

1:1

Connect letters and sounds

digraphs
trigraphs
vowel teams
blends
word families
inflections
syllable types
roots/affixes
word origin

Orthography

For All Phases of Word Recognition: Build and Extend Vocabuage and Oral Language

As we have emphasized throughout LETRS, the oral language foundations for reading and writing must be stimulated continuously in classroom instruction. Students who are familiar with the meanings of the words and phrases they are starting to read will have an easier time developing reading proficiency. Syntax (sentence structure) and semantics (word and phrase meanings) in written text can be processed only if those aspects of language are known in spoken language.

For instance, Pikulski and Chard (2005) provide an example of two words: **zigzags** and **onychophagia** (nail-biting). The first word is easy for mature readers to decode despite the fact that it is considered a rare word in printed English. But the second word is difficult for even mature readers. Why? It, too, is rare in printed English like the first word, but it is also rare in speech and, thus, unlikely to be in a mature reader's mental lexicon. If a reader is not able to connect a printed word with its sound, use, and meaning, it is unlikely to be decoded fluently (Pikulski & Chard, p. 514).

Integrating Vocabulary Elaboration

Knowing the multiple meanings of words (e.g., **lap**, **bat**, **miss**, **deck**) as soon as they can decode them helps students recognize the words more quickly (Wolf & Katzir-Cohen, 2001). Retrieval of a word from memory is easier when multiple associations are connected to that word. Using a multiple-meaning map (introduced in LETRS Module 4), the teacher elicits from students several meanings for a word. Various meanings are recalled and used in picture-matching games and sentence-generation activities. The words are read in multiple-meaning stories constructed to stimulate students' semantic flexibility.

Examples:

BAT	LAP
Sam went up to **bat**. He had on a **Batman** hat.	The girl is in Santa's **lap**. The cat **laps** his milk. The water **laps** onto the shore. The horse is running **laps** around the track.

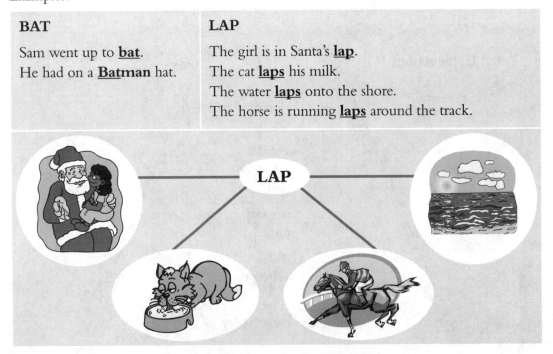

Teaching the Phrasing Indicated by Punctuation

Excerpt 1: "Alphabetic Prosody" from *50 Nifty Activities* (Dodson, 2008)

Fluency

Alphabetic Prosody

Activity Overview

One definition of reading fluency is "accurate reading at a minimal rate with appropriate prosodic features (expression)" (Hudson, Mercer, & Lane, 2000). Prosodic features refer to punctuation and phrasing. Fluent readers read in phrases, using the intonation and prosodic features of the text, therefore reading with appropriate expression.

Automaticity occurs when a skill is performed so easily that it is done without conscious attention. Alphabetic Prosody is an activity that can help students learn to pay attention to punctuation marks and understand what they represent, rapidly and automatically. Once students have mastered the meaning of the punctuation marks, they can transfer that automatic knowledge to sentences and connected text quite easily.

Materials • • • • • •

- Card stock printed with single letters of the alphabet
- Marker
- Plastic sheet protectors
- Student whiteboards, dry-erase markers, and erasers

Whole Classroom Instruction

Set the purpose. Say: "Paying attention to punctuation marks will help you to read with expression. When you read with expression, it is a sign that you understand what you are reading. This activity will give you practice reading punctuation marks."

Prior to the activity, take the card stock printed with single letters and punctuate the letters with punctuation that has been previously taught, for example, **A! A? A.** Place the letter cards in plastic sheet protectors and arrange in alphabetical order.

1. Remind students what an exclamation mark means and how to read it when they encounter one.

2. Read the letters **A!, B!,** and **C!** to the class with a lot of excitement.

3. Ask the class to say the next two or three letters with you: "**D!, E!, F!,** and **G!**"

4. Ask the class to read the next set of letters in unison without you: "**H!, I!, J!, K!**"

5. Repeat this activity with other graphemes and add other punctuation marks (like question marks and periods) that have been taught.

Fluency Alphabetic Prosody

75

Return to the purpose. Say:
"You've been practicing paying attention to punctuation marks. Punctuation marks will help you to read with expression. When you read with expression, it is a sign that you understand what you are reading."

Small Group Work

1. Say a sound and ask students to write the letter(s) (grapheme) for that sound on their whiteboards.

2. Repeat the sound in an excited way and ask students to add the punctuation mark after the letter(s) that makes the reader know it needs to be read in an excited manner.

3. Have students say the sound with expression as they write it and then again when they are finished writing the exclamation mark.

4. Say several sounds with excitement and ask students to write the letter(s) and use the correct punctuation mark. For instance, say "/sh!/" and have students write **sh!**

5. Repeat this process with other punctuation marks that students have been taught.

6. Give the group a simple sentence to copy onto their whiteboards. For example: **The dog barked.**

   ℮ Have them read it as a simple declarative sentence with a period at the end: **"The dog barked."**

   ℮ Then ask them to change the period to a question mark and read the sentence again: **"The dog barked?"**

   ℮ Finally, have them change the question mark to an exclamation mark and read it in an excited manner: **"The dog barked!"**

Independent Practice

Alphabetic Prosody can be repeated with students working in pairs.

1. Have each partner write out the first eight letters of the alphabet on their whiteboard and put punctuation marks in between the letters. Examples: **A, B, C, D. E! F! G? H.**

2. Ask the partners to take turns reading each other's alphabet. Students can repeat this step with another set of alphabet letters or with the entire alphabet if time allows.

3. Next, tell the partners to work together to choose simple words and phrases with different punctuation marks and to write them on their whiteboards. When they finish writing, have them read the words and phrases aloud together: **"Dog! Dog? Dog."**

Stretching Students' Learning

◉ Students can practice Alphabetic Prosody using sentences and short passages they create themselves. They can share them with another student and read each other's punctuation marks.

Exercise 2.2 | Practice Alphabetic Prosody

- Partner up. Each of you will write out a string of 8–10 letters, with punctuation marks inserted to help the reader read with appropriate expression.
- Ask your partner to read your alphabet sentence with the expression indicated by each punctuation mark.

Early Alphabetic Phase: Automaticity With Letters, Sounds, and Sound-Symbol Correspondence

Letter knowledge (including letter-naming fluency), phonemic awareness, and knowledge of phoneme-grapheme correspondence are the foundations for building fluency in printed word recognition. These early skills can be addressed in a variety of ways, but the best methods and programs provide a systematic, explicit scope and sequence of instruction so that students' learning of the alphabetic code is not left to chance (Ehri, 2004).

Each of the following activities are from cumulative, systematic, research-supported programs that provide fluency practice after young students are taught letter names (*Excerpt 2*) and phoneme segmentation (*Excerpt 3*).

Excerpt 2: "Letter Name Practice" from *Stepping Stones to Literacy*
(Nelson, Cooper, & Gonzalez, 2004)

[Handwritten margin notes: Activities for Early Alphabetical Fluency Kindergarten Identify letters in one minute]

Letter Name Practice

1. **"Today we practice saying the letter names fast."**

   "Hoy vamos a practicar diciendo los nombres de letras rápidamente."

2. **"Point to the letter, and say its name."**

   "Señalen la letra y díganme el nombre de la letra."

   Make it a game-like format (e.g., "Let's see how many letters you can name in one minute."). (e.g., "Veamos cuántas letras que ustedes pueden nombrar en un minuto.") Attempt to get the children to practice several times.

	H	o	G	h	o
5	G	c	H	o	g
10	G	d	O	G	c
15	H	g	N	H	o
20	D	H	O	G	H
25	G	h	C	o	O
30	G	n	H	o	d
35	H	c	O	G	N
40	H	o	G	H	O
45	G	d	H	O	C

Lesson 10 – Page 199

Excerpt 3: "Phonemic Awareness—Phoneme Segmentation" from *Practicing Basic Skills in Reading: One-Minute Fluency Builders Series* (Beck, Anderson, & Conrad, 2008)

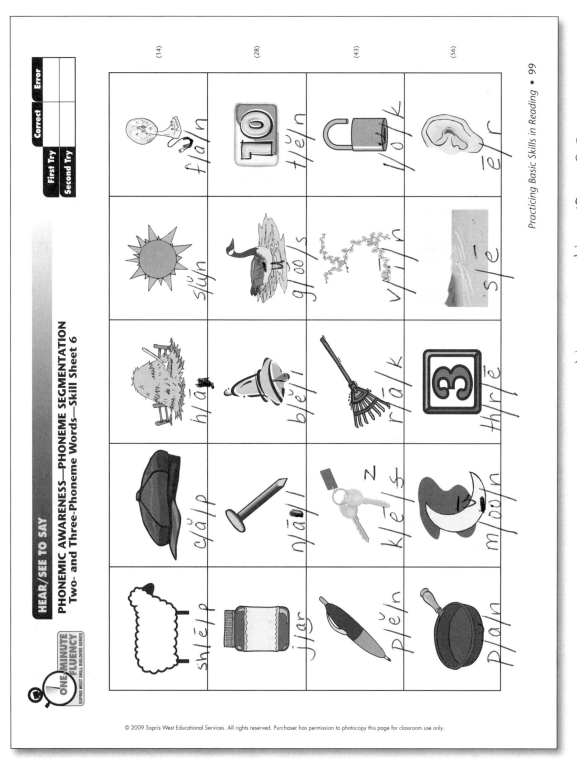

Practicing Basic Skills in Reading • 99

In one minute tell you the name of item &
segment into sound

three th-r-ee
sheep- sh-ee-p
hay- h-ay
sun s-u-n
hat h-a-t

Most systematic programs also include routines for practicing phoneme-grapheme (or grapheme-phoneme) associations. In *Exercise 2.3*, we will rapidly recall the most common graphemes for the phonemes taught in LETRS Module 3.

Exercise 2.3 | Phoneme-Grapheme Association

- Your presenter will time you for 1 minute.
- In that time, write as many standard graphemes for each of the following phonemes as you can recall from Module 3. (You may write single letters or letter combinations.)

Consonant Phonemes	Grapheme(s)	Consonant Phonemes	Grapheme(s)
/p/	p	/th/	th
/b/	b	/th/	th
/m/	m, mn, mb	/sh/	sh, ch
/t/	t, ed, tt putt	/zh/	ti,
/d/	d, ed	/ch/	ch,
/n/	n, kn, gn	/j/	j
/k/	lk, ck, c, k ch, que qu	/l/	l
/g/	g	/r/	r
/ng/	ng	/y/	y
/f/	ph, f	/w/	w, wh
/v/	v, ve	/wh/	wh
/s/	s,	/h/	h, wh
/z/	s, z		

(continued)

Exercise 2.3 (continued)

Vowel Phonemes	Grapheme(s)	Vowel Phonemes	Grapheme(s)
/ē/	ea, ee, ie,	/ō/	
/ĭ/	i,	/ŏŏ/	
/ā/	a-e, eigh, ai	/ū/	
/ĕ/	e,	/yū/	
/ă/	a au	/oi/	
/ī/	igh, ie,	/ou/	
/ŏ/	o au	/er/	
/ŭ/	ough u	/ar/	
/aw/	aw, au	/or/	

Early to Later Alphabetic Phase: Automaticity With Phonic Decoding

As phoneme-grapheme and grapheme-phoneme correspondences are being learned, students also should practice "sounding out" fluently, using learned correspondences, and spelling words by their sounds. Reading nonsense words—which are often syllables in real words that will be read later—is one form of practice. Reading decodable text with many examples of the words and patterns that have been taught is another way of developing phonic decoding fluency. Fast recall of graphemes for phonemes as well as spelling words using phoneme-grapheme mapping (Grace, 2006) are also effective practices.

Decodable text is constructed to provide a novice reader with practice using sound-symbol associations and sound-blending skills that have previously been taught (refer to *Excerpts 4 and 5*). Decodable text contains a high proportion (usually 80–90 percent) of words that use known phonic patterns, along with a few high-frequency words with odd spellings that have also been previously taught. Decodable text requires students to use learned word-attack skills instead of guessing at words from context or pictures. Although a student at this phase may still exert considerable mental effort to read words, the practice afforded by decodable text will eventually lead to automatic word recognition.

Excerpt 4: Example of Decodable Text from *Power Readers* (Ebbers, 2007)

The sun felt hot. Tim, Nick, and Pug went to the pond.

8

Tim dug his hand into the sand. Nick dug his cup into the sand.

9

Look up these books.

Excerpt 5: Example of Decodable Text from *Practicing Basic Skills in Reading: One-Minute Fluency Builders Series* (Beck, Anderson, & Conrad, 2008)

SEE TO SAY

READING PASSAGES
First Grade Level—Skill Sheet 13
Directions: Say each word. If you finish before the end of the timing, go back to the beginning and start over.

ONE-MINUTE FLUENCY
SOPRIS WEST SKILL BUILDERS SERIES

	Correct	Error
First Try		
Second Try		

Meg's bed is bumpy and lumpy. Dizzy, the itty-bitty (9)

bunny, is in the bed. (14)

Off, Dizzy! Off the bed! No pets in bed. (23)

Dot's crib is lumpy and bumpy. Zap is a kitty. The (34)

kitty is in the crib. Off, Zap, off the crib! No pets (46)

in bed. (48)

Pug is in Tim's bed. Tim's bed is muddy and dusty. (59)

Pug is a pig. (63)

Get off, Pug! Get the pig off the bed! No pets in bed. (76)

No lumpy, bumpy, dusty, pets in bed! (83)

Practicing Basic Skills in Reading • 341

Decodable texts fit a specific scope and sequence that should be identified for consumers. One example of a beginning scope and sequence of phonics instruction is outlined by Moats and Farrell (2007):

- High-utility single consonants (e.g., **f, s, m, t, p**) and a short vowel (e.g., /ă/, /ĕ/, /ŏ/);
- High-frequency "heart" words—irregularly spelled words that need to be learned "by heart" (e.g., **was, said, of**), 3–5 per week;
- All single consonants;
- All short vowels;
- Consonant oddities (e.g., **x, qu**);
- Consonant digraphs (e.g., **ch, sh, th, wh, -ck**);
- Double final consonants (**f, l, s**, and **z**);
- Consonant blends, final and initial;
- Inflectional suffixes (e.g., **-s, -es, -ed, -ing**);
- Hard and soft **c** and **g**;
- Trigraphs (e.g., **-tch, -dge**); and
- Common rime patterns or "chunks" (e.g., **-ink, -ank, -unk; -all; -ing**).

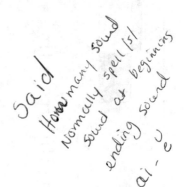

Said — How many sound — Normally spell /s/ — Sound at beginning — ending sound — ai – e

Later Alphabetic Phase: Recognizing High-Frequency Words

High-frequency words are those that occur most often in written language. Some are regular, some are irregular, and some partially irregular (see LETRS Module 3 for a full discussion of English spelling patterns). Irregular and odd spellings are disproportionately represented in the highest-frequency words. Most irregular, high-frequency words include at least some letter-sound regularities that can help students learn words. In addition, if students know regular patterns of correspondence, identifying what is irregular can help them remember words. Eventually, all known words must be known by sight, but extra practice is often needed on those words that are not pattern-based. Speed drills, flash cards, and computer-based practice play a role in increasing automatic recognition of high-frequency irregular words.

Excerpt 6, from Adams and Brown (2007b), illustrates how a speed drill can be constructed.

[handwritten: a g a i n (in boxes)]

[handwritten: how many sounds ← shorter ← ă g ai n]

[handwritten: how do we spell /g/ /n/]

[handwritten: tricky parts — have a heart about it]

Excerpt 6: Example of High-Frequency Word Speed Drill from *The Six-Minute Solution (Primary Level)* (Adams & Brown, 2007b)

PRIMARY AUTOMATIC WORDS BY TENS

List 4

0	which	one	you	were	her
5	all	she	there	would	their
10	which	one	you	were	her
15	all	she	there	would	their
20	which	one	you	were	her
25	all	she	there	would	their
30	which	one	you	were	her
35	all	she	there	would	their
40	which	one	you	were	her
45	all	she	there	would	their
50	which	one	you	were	her
55	all	she	there	would	their
60					

236 The Six-Minute Solution: A Reading Fluency Program (Primary Level)

how far they can read when 1 min is up

Read whole list in 1 minute

Later Alphabetic to Consolidated Alphabetic Phase: Rimes, Roots, and Affixes

Moving students from letter-sound knowledge to recognition of larger linguistic units (e.g., rimes, syllables, morphemes) is important for building fluency in word recognition and can facilitate students' transition from the fully alphabetic phase to the consolidated alphabetic phase.

Ehri listed the most common rime patterns and affixes (i.e., prefixes and suffixes) that occur in English words (Ehri, 1997, p. 165; originally calculated by Wylie & Durrell, 1970):

Common Rimes in Single-Syllable English Words						
-ack	-all	-ain	-ake	-ale	-ame	-an
-ank	-ap	-ash	-at	-ate	-aw	-ay
-eat	-ell	-est	-ice	-ick	-ide	-ight
-ill	-in	-ine	-ing	-ink	-ip	-ir
-ock	-oke	-op	-ore	-or	-uck	-ug
-ump	-unk					

Common English Affixes						
com-	con-	de-	dis-	ex-	im-	in-
pre-	pro-	re-	un-	-al	-able	-ate
-ant	-ed	-en	-er	-ent	-or	-ize
-ist	-ing	-ive	-ite	-ion	-ic	-ful
-ly	-less	-ment	-ness	-ous		

Maryanne Wolf's *RAVE-O* program (Wolf, 2003), deliberately and systematically emphasizes direct instruction of inflections (e.g., **-ed**, **-s**, **-ing**, **-er**, **-est**) and common suffixes as soon as students have mastered basic phonic associations. Called "ender benders," these inflections and suffixes are studied both in isolation and in combination with base words. Wolf and others (Berninger & Richards, 2002) contend that even the poorest readers should be taught from the outset to recognize and understand beginning-level morphology.

Excerpts 7 and 8, from *The Six-Minute Solution* (Adams & Brown, 2007a, 2007c), demonstrate this principle of intervention with intermediate- and secondary-level students.

Excerpt 7: Example of Prefix Speed Drill from *The Six-Minute Solution (Intermediate Level)* (Adams & Brown, 2007a)

SET 3

Prefixes (en-, em-, non-, over-, mis-)

0	en	em	non	over	mis
5	mis	over	non	em	en
10	non	en	mis	over	em
15	over	non	en	mis	em
20	em	mis	non	en	over
25	non	en	over	em	mis
30	en	em	non	over	mis
35	mis	over	non	em	en
40	non	en	mis	over	em
45	over	non	en	mis	em
50	em	mis	non	en	over
55	non	en	over	em	mis
60					

Prefixes (en-, em-, non-, over-, mis-) With Words

0	enable	encode	enclose	enforce	enlarge
5	employ	embark	embattle	embroil	embed
10	nonfiction	nonstop	nonslip	nonliving	nondrip
15	overact	overfill	overpay	overdo	overload
20	mislead	misorder	misname	misread	mistreat
25	enable	encode	enclose	enforce	enlarge
30	employ	embark	embattle	embroil	embed
35	nonfiction	nonstop	nonslip	nonliving	nondrip
40	overact	overfill	overpay	overdo	overload
45	mislead	misorder	misname	misread	mistreat
50	enable	encode	enclose	enforce	enlarge
55	employ	embark	embattle	embroil	embed
60					

Excerpt 8: Example of Suffix Speed Drill from *The Six-Minute Solution (Secondary Level)* (Adams & Brown, 2007c)

SET 1

Suffixes (-ed, -ing, -ly, -er, -or)

0	ed	ing	ly	er	or
5	or	er	ly	ing	ed
10	ly	ed	er	or	ing
15	ing	or	ed	ly	er
20	er	ly	or	ed	ing
25	ed	ing	ly	er	or
30	or	er	ly	ing	ed
35	ly	ed	er	or	ing
40	ing	or	ed	ly	er
45	er	ly	or	ed	ing
50	ed	ing	ly	er	or
55	or	er	ly	ing	ed
60					

SET 2

Suffixes (-ed, -ing, -ly, -er, -or) With Words

0	caved	chimed	jammed	smiled	used
5	fixing	matching	saying	wishing	floating
10	softly	quietly	nicely	loudly	quickly
15	banker	flier	painter	teacher	farmer
20	actor	sailor	visitor	governor	senator
25	caved	chimed	jammed	smiled	used
30	fixing	matching	saying	wishing	floating
35	softly	quietly	nicely	loudly	quickly
40	banker	flier	painter	teacher	farmer
45	actor	sailor	visitor	governor	senator
50	caved	chimed	jammed	smiled	used
55	fixing	matching	saying	wishing	floating
60					

Teaching, Modeling, and Practicing Using a Word-Recognition Strategy During Text Reading

Students who are moving from later alphabetic reading to the fully consolidated alphabetic phase but who are not yet automatic with word recognition need to practice applying what they know about the code during reading itself. We suggest the following four-step cueing routine for approaching an unknown word:

1. "Look carefully at the word. Identify the parts you know."[2]
2. "Sound out the word."
3. Check understanding by asking, "Does it sound right?"
4. Tweak student pronunciation, if necessary.
5. Check with somebody make sure you are right

Consolidation: Transferring Skills to Text Reading

Hiebert (2005) taught reading to a treatment group of intermediate-age students using texts that included several unique features, including only a few unfamiliar vocabulary words and a high percentage of high-frequency words, spelled both regularly and irregularly. Thus, the texts were structured to provide concentrated practice on selected words (e.g., "The Rights of Citizens" excerpt below) and to provide multiple short selections that used the same vocabulary. Students in the treatment condition reading the specially designed controlled vocabulary made significantly greater gains in fluency than students in uncontrolled commercial texts.

The Rights of Citizens

You are a citizen of your school. You are also a citizen of your town, state, and country. Citizens in the United States have rights. Rights are the things you can do. No one can take away your rights as a citizen.

You have the right to go to school. You have the right to go to the park or ride on a bus. When you grow up, you will have the right to vote. People in the United States have the right to vote for anyone they choose.

—Hiebert (2003)

Texts can be structured to provide multiple exposures to the same words. Provision of multiple exposures to specific words and spelling patterns is one of the most important features of well-designed beginning reading programs. It is important to look carefully at the content of "leveled" books, because they may not provide as much practice with specific words as many students need.

---

[2] This simplified direction is meant to direct students' attention to familiar graphemes, syllables, and morphemes. However, this direction can be misleading in some cases, as in the word **mother**. **Moth** is not the first syllable of this word, and students would have to tweak the pronunciation to recover **mother** from the recognizable parts.

In Chapter 3, we explore and role-play proven strategies for fluency-oriented instruction. No matter which instructional activities are used, fluency practice should always lead to some kind of connection with meaning.

Take 2 Review: Create a Speed Drill

- Teachers can design their own speed drills for use with individual students or with small groups of 3–5 students (Adams & Brown, 2007; Dodson, 2008). Prepare a grid in which five to ten learned words or word parts are randomly placed across five columns and 10–12 rows (refer to sample grid below). Grid components may consist of:
  - irregular, high-frequency words that students can read accurately;
  - pattern-based words whose sounds are known;
  - common syllables, rime patterns, letter combinations, or morphemes that are known; or
  - important words for academic reading that have been previously taught.
- Role-play the following steps with each student:
  1. Ask the student (or each student in the small group) to read the words or word parts for accuracy, without timing.
  2. Tell the student (or each student in the small group) to practice individually to prepare for a timing.
  3. Time each student reading the speed drill.
  4. Ask each student to talk about the meaning of one of the words, to locate a word by its meaning, or to use a word in a sentence.

Chapter 3

Improving Fluency in Each Tier of Instruction

Learner Objectives for Chapter 3
- Become familiar with fluency norms.
- Identify, observe, and practice fluency-building techniques for whole-class instruction.
- Identify, observe, and practice fluency-building techniques for students with reading problems.

Warm-Up: Review Norms for Oral Reading Fluency (ORF) by Grade Level and Reading Level
- Review the Hasbrouck and Tindal (2005) ORF norms[2] for the range of words correct per minute (WCPM) scores (*Table 3.1*, next page) that are typical for students in grades 1–8. These norms are based on samples of thousands of students at each level (notice "count" data) and have been replicated by others. The norms were obtained by asking students to read from unrehearsed, grade-level text.
- Answer these questions in your discussion:

  1. Do students typically lose fluency over the summer months? _____
     - Why might this happen? _____

       _____

  2. At what grade levels do gains in fluency level off?_____

     _____

     - What does this suggest in terms of assessment and instruction in reading?

       _____

       _____

---

[2] Note: These ORF norms are downloadable from http://brt.uoregon.edu/techreports/TR_33_NCORF_ DescStats.pdf or http://www.brtprojects.org/techreports/TR_33_NCORF_DescStats.pdf

3. Select one grade level, and compare a student who is at the 10th percentile with a student at the 90th percentile. If each student reads 10 minutes per day, what might be the approximate difference in the number of words read in a 30-week school year?

has lower #'s than Dibels

Dibels by 3rd grade can they read + comprehend Silently

Table 3.1   Oral Reading Fluency (ORF) Norms
(Hasbrouck & Tindal, 2005)

GRADE	PERCENTILE	FALL WCPM	WINTER WCPM	SPRING WCPM
1	90		81	111
	75		47	82
	50		23	53
	25		12	28
	10		6	15
	SD		32	39
	Count		16,950	19,434
2	90	106	125	142
	75	79	100	117
	50	51	72	89
	25	25	42	61
	10	11	18	31
	SD	37	41	42
	Count	15,896	18,229	20,128
3	90	128	146	162
	75	99	120	137
	50	71	92	107
	25	44	62	78
	10	21	36	48
	SD	40	43	44
	Count	16,988	17,383	18,372

GRADE	PERCENTILE	FALL WCPM	WINTER WCPM	SPRING WCPM
4	90	145	166	180
	75	119	139	152
	50	94	112	123
	25	68	87	98
	10	45	61	72
	SD	40	41	43
	Count	16,523	14,572	16,269
5	90	166	182	194
	75	139	156	168
	50	110	127	139
	25	85	99	109
	10	61	74	83
	SD	45	44	45
	Count	16,212	13,331	15,292
6	90	177	195	204
	75	153	167	177
	50	127	140	150
	25	98	111	122
	10	68	82	93
	SD	42	45	44
	Count	10,520	9,218	11,290
7	90	180	192	202
	75	156	165	177
	50	128	136	150
	25	102	109	123
	10	79	88	98
	SD	40	43	41
	Count	6,482	4,058	5,998
8	90	185	199	199
	75	161	173	177
	50	133	146	151
	25	106	115	124
	10	77	84	97
	SD	43	45	41
	Count	5,546	3,496	5,335

WCPM: The number of words read correctly per minute
SD: Standard deviation
COUNT: Number of students assessed

Fluency-Oriented Reading Instruction for Tier 1 (Whole Class)

One of the five essential components of reading instruction supported by reading research (Chard, Vaughn, & Tyler, 2002; NICHD, 2000; Pikulski & Chard, 2005), text-reading fluency can be developed through a variety of techniques. As illustrated in *Figure 3.1*, the emphasis of instruction and choice of techniques will vary somewhat for each tier of instruction in a multitiered organizational system.

Figure 3.1. Three-Tier Model for Reading Instruction
(developed by the University of Texas)

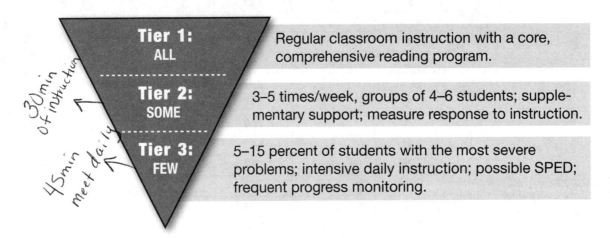

30min of instruction

45min meet daily

Tier 1: ALL — Regular classroom instruction with a core, comprehensive reading program.

Tier 2: SOME — 3–5 times/week, groups of 4–6 students; supplementary support; measure response to instruction.

Tier 3: FEW — 5–15 percent of students with the most severe problems; intensive daily instruction; possible SPED; frequent progress monitoring.

To review (from LETRS Module 1), Tier 1 reading instruction is delivered to the whole class and addresses all essential components in appropriate balance for that grade level. Approximately 2–2.5 hours daily at first and second grade are necessary to implement a comprehensive reading program, which includes a combination of teacher-directed and student-directed activities as well as a mix of code-emphasis and meaning-emphasis instruction. The proportion of each instruction component may be adjusted according to the needs of the students in the class (Connor, Morrison, & Katch, 2004).

As described by Stahl and Heubach (2005), fluency-oriented reading instruction can be accomplished with adjustments to core, comprehensive reading program (CCRP) materials. Those adjustments include incorporating the following elements:

- Partner-reading
- Repeated readings of texts in the CCRP
- Monitored "choice" reading during the day
- Independent (home) reading time that is monitored and rewarded

Fluency-oriented, whole-classroom instruction is especially valuable at the second-grade level, where Stahl and Heubach (2005) demonstrated its positive effects. In the context of Chall's (1996) stage model, the acquisition of text-reading fluency is an important segue between learning to decode (i.e., learning to read) and reading independently for comprehension (i.e., reading to learn). At second and third grade, students are acquiring a larger sight-reading vocabulary and are consolidating various reading skills. This is the stage in which students increase the volume of their daily reading considerably, develop more confidence as independent readers, and commonly get "hooked" on series books by the same author. Series books provide extensive reading practice that is motivated by students' familiarity with characters, a setting, a story line, and an author's predictable style.

Alternate Oral Reading With a Partner

Partner-reading increases the amount of reading students do during the day while freeing the teacher to work with individuals or small groups. Partner-reading allows students to support one another as they enjoy reading in pairs or in threes. Partner-reading is often a student favorite in the literacy block. Peer-assisted learning strategies (PALS; Mathes, Torgesen, Allen, & Allor, 2001) constitute a research-supported, structured way of teaching students to work productively as reading partners.

[handwritten margin note: good for 2nd-3rd grade... Use narrative/ expository questions...]

Establishing Reading Partners

Stahl and Heubach (2005) allowed second-grade students to select their own partners. Friends selected one another and, reportedly, conflicts were few among the students in their study. A related study (Meisinger, Schwanenflugel, Bradley, & Stahl, 2004) also recommended allowing students to choose their own partners, with some teacher direction.

The PALS (Mathes et al., 2001) approach is more prescriptive. It ensures that the poorer readers are paired with students who read somewhat better than they do, but that students are reasonably well-matched. The steps involved in this more directive approach are:

1. Rank the group according to reading ability. Consider eliminating highly proficient readers, students with learning disabilities, and students with emotional handicaps from this activity. Assign them to other activities.
2. Divide the remaining group in half.
3. Assign pairs by matching the top reader on the top half of the list with the top reader on the bottom half of the list and so forth. These pairings are likely to be close enough in reading ability that the students can work well together.
4. Check the pairings, and change any that might not be compatible.

Selecting Text of Appropriate Difficulty

Stahl and Heubach (2005) reported that students in their classrooms tended to choose books that were at, or slightly more difficult than, their instructional level (90–95 percent accurate). The students also tended to benefit instructionally from more difficult materials than generally assumed, especially when support and scaffolding were available. This finding contradicts the more common recommendation that students work with material at their independent reading levels (95 percent or better correct). To incorporate structure into text selection, a teacher may choose several texts from previous reading lessons that are within the students' instructional reading levels, and allow students to choose from those texts. Teacher supervision of reading materials ensures that students will select materials they can read and will benefit from the partner-reading assignment as intended.

One caution, however. Students who are far below grade level will need to practice with text material well within their instructional range; they may not be able to handle grade-level text during fluency practice.

Modeling and Teaching the Partner-Reading Procedure

Teachers should show students what to do when they read with a partner. Explicitly assigning and defining roles puts students at ease. We recommend that teachers show students how to follow these steps before they engage in partner-reading:

1. Start by selecting a student with whom to model the process. Sit side-by-side and hold the book/text together. Ask other students to observe what you and your student partner are doing.

   - Assign the roles of "Reader" and "Coach." Take the role of Coach.
   - Ask the Reader to select a book/text and to read a section—a paragraph, a page, a chapter, or the whole book. (The reading selection should be agreed to ahead of time.) The Coach follows along and watches/listens for mistakes. When a mistake occurs, the Coach either provides the correct word or asks the Reader to check the word and try again. After the book/text selection is read, partners return to the beginning of the book or story. Page by page or section by section, the Coach asks the Reader to tell what happened or to recall what each part was about.

2. Exchange roles with the student Reader and model again. Remind the Coach (now the student) what to say when a mistake is made, and role-play making mistakes. Demonstrate reading at a comfortable speed, reading with expression, and understanding what is read. When you finish reading the book/text, return to the beginning and have the Coach ask you what each page or section was about.

3. Assign roles to all other pairs of students. Reader 1 (Reader) should be the stronger reader and should read first, while Reader 2 (Coach) listens, follows the text, corrects mistakes, and conducts the comprehension check. Remind the Coaches that they may prompt the Readers by saying, "Check that word," before they provide the correct word.

   - Reader 2 (Coach) then picks up where Reader 1 (Reader) stops reading, and the roles are reversed.
   - After the book/text is read, Reader 1 asks Reader 2 to look at each page and answer the question, "What happened here?"

4. Direct the student pairs to keep a log of books/texts they read to earn points for reading, following well, and cooperating with their partner. To add summarizing or retelling to the activity, ask each student pair to share what they read with another student pair.

Exercise 3.1 — Role-Play and View a Video Demonstration of Partner-Reading

- In groups of three—Teacher, Coach, and Reader—role-play the four-step procedure just outlined.

Video Demonstration

(*Teaching Reading Essentials* [Moats & Farrell, 2007], Part 3, Demonstration 22)

- Watch the video, then answer these questions.

1. What does the teacher do to explain the activity?

   _____

   _____

2. Does the second pair of students know what to do after the explanation?

   _____

   _____

3. Would they need more explanation or supervision to maintain appropriate behavior?

   _____

   _____

[handwritten: Whisper Read / mark where you stopped...]

[handwritten: 1. Accuracy / 2. Partner / 3. Time it]

Repeated Reading   *[handwritten: Read up to 4 times]*

Repeated reading techniques are not new (Carreker, 2005; Meyer, 2002; Samuels, 1997). They are intended to increase reading speed, enhance comprehension, and enable students to become independent and self-confident readers. Guided, repeated oral reading was found to be effective by the National Reading Panel's (NICHD, 2000) meta-analysis of existing research.

The method is straightforward and usually improves fluency, accuracy, and comprehension in students who are ready to benefit from oral reading fluency practice. The standard procedure is as follows (Meyer, 2002):

1. The teacher ensures that the reading material is at the appropriate level of difficulty (90–95 percent accuracy). The teacher previews the topic and vocabulary with the student so that the student is focused on the meaning of the text.

2. The student gets ready to read the text orally while the teacher sets a 1-minute or 2-minute timer. (In order to encourage a student to read the text all the way through, the teacher may say, "Mark your paper," at the 1-minute juncture but allow the student to keep reading until he reaches a good stopping point. Then, WCPM can be calculated when the reading is completed.) The student graphs his first 1- or 2-minute WCPM on the text reading. (Students should graph their own results whenever possible.)

[handwritten: Pick an emotion when reading the story...]

3. Within a day or two, the student reads the same text three to four times for practice, with or without self-timing. (More than three or four readings is generally not beneficial.) The student may read to an adult or a partner or into a tape recorder.

4. The timed WCPM procedure is repeated. As a rule of thumb, a 10 percent gain from first to final (i.e., three to four) readings is used as a target for improvement (e.g., a student should improve from 60 WCPM to 66 WCPM with this practice). If the student gains about 10 percent or better in WCPM, the text should be changed to a more challenging level. If the student does not make the desired gain—an unusual occurrence if the text selection is appropriate—an easier text may be selected or more previewing may be used. (Appropriate goals for weekly improvement on first readings can be estimated on the basis of curriculum-based measurement research [Fuchs, Fuchs, Hamlett, Walz, & Germann, 1993], summarized in *Table 3.2* below.)

Table 3.2. Expected Rate of WCPM Increase by Week

Grade Level	Realistic Goal	Ambitious Goal
1	2.0	3.0
2	1.5	2.0
3	1.0	1.5
4	.85	1.1
5	.5	.8
6	.3	.65

5. The student then reads another passage at the same level of difficulty until that target rate is attained again. The teacher or partner gives feedback on word-recognition errors. Usually, practice on the first passage transfers to improvement on initial reading of the second passage and a faster rate of gain with repeated readings.

6. Results are graphed (refer to graph example). The teacher should conduct spot checks on comprehension to make sure the student is reading for meaning.

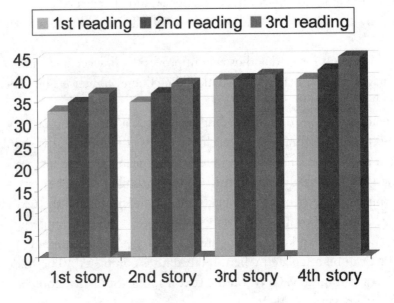

Over a period of eight to ten weeks of frequent, distributed practice, a student's average weekly score should improve. In addition, rate and accuracy scores should increase on the first readings of unfamiliar text over time, reflecting the generalization of improved reading skills. The benefits of repeated readings of any specific text usually generalize to the readings of new texts. That is why there is no additional payoff for reading one text over and over.

To summarize, fluency growth is not facilitated by memorizing text, pushing to read as fast as possible for the sake of speed, or repeating a reading more than four times.

Monitored "Choice" Reading

Well-stocked classroom libraries and school libraries, with books catalogued and organized by readability level and topic, are essential for promoting reading. Students who are at grade level or above are the ones who may benefit most from in-school reading of books of their choosing.

Monitored choice reading, however, is more structured than "Drop Everything and Read" (DEAR). Teachers check with students to keep track of what they are reading and help students find books at an appropriate level. Periodically, students are asked to retell, evaluate, or report on the books of their choice. Most importantly, choice reading does not interfere with or replace teacher-directed instruction.

Home or Independent Reading Time

Parents, family members, and other caregivers can participate in promoting reading at home by:

- limiting the amount of time the child spends watching television and playing video games;
- establishing a family reading routine at a certain time of day;
- monitoring and signing off on the child's independent reading log;
- talking to the child about her reading;
- getting a library card and visiting the library with the child;
- sharing read-alouds at home; and
- participating in incentive programs that are promoted by the school or community.

occasionally do a re-tell have 1 min to retell what your read...

©Cartoonbank.com

"Dumbledore smiled, his eyes twinkling."

Fluency Instruction for Students Who Are Below Benchmark (Tiers 2 and 3)

Subtypes of Poor Readers

Students who are below benchmark in oral reading fluency (approximately 40th percentile) after the end of first grade represent several types of struggling readers (see *Figure 3.2*).

Figure 3.2. Diagram of Subtypes of Reading Disability

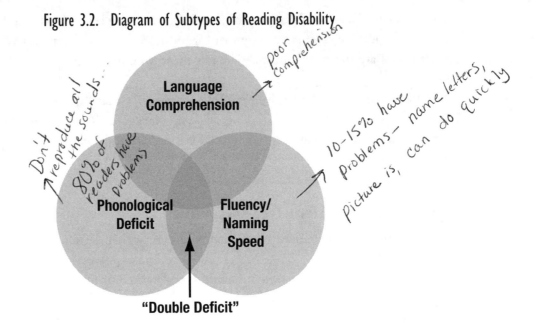

Handwritten annotations: Don't reproduce all the sounds... • 80% of readers have problems • poor comprehension • 10-15% have problems – name letters, picture is, can do quickly

English-speaking students with reading difficulties can be grouped, theoretically, into at least three distinct subgroups (Fletcher, Lyon, Fuchs, & Barnes, 2007; Katzir et al., 2006; Wolf & Katzir-Cohen, 2001):

1. *Those with weaknesses in phonologically based decoding skills.* Most students who are poor readers are weak in decoding and word recognition because of weaknesses in underlying phonological skills including phoneme identification, recall, manipulation, and memory. Their word-reading is usually inaccurate on tests such as the Test of Word Reading Efficiency (TOWRE; Torgesen, Wagner, & Rashotte, 1999), and they have trouble on phonological awareness and memory tests.

2. *Those with slow or dysfluent reading.* These students may be accurate in sound-recognition and blending but are slow to recognize letter patterns and words and to store words in memory for automatic recognition. They are slow on rapid automatized naming (RAN; see example) and rapid alternating stimulus (RAS) tests (Wolf & Denckla, 2005). They may be accurate but slow on measures such as TOWRE (Torgesen et al., 1999). Their difficulties may be attributable to either the brain's ability to store whole-word orthographic images or to the brain's timing mechanisms or ability to coordinate processing systems.

Example of Rapid Automatized Naming (RAN) Reading Exercise				
o	d	g	a	b
g	b	d	o	a
a	o	b	g	d
b	a	o	d	g
d	g	a	b	o

If students have phonological processing weaknesses and slow processing on RAN tests, they are known as "double deficit" students (Wolf & Bowers, 2000), the most difficult to teach and the slowest to improve. They respond best to a multicomponent approach, delivered intensively.

3. *Those with language comprehension problems.* These students are slow and/or inaccurate in building connections among sounds, words, meanings, and ideas. Some are particularly weak in understanding sentence meanings. These students may read without appropriate expression, or prosody. Some read inaccurately and quickly, including students who are impulsive, overactive, or lacking in self-monitoring skills. They may rush through reading without thinking about or understanding what they read. They may have a high error rate in timed readings because they are not processing the meaning of what they are reading. Their instruction should emphasize comprehension at the word, phrase, sentence, and paragraph levels, in addition to an emphasis on reading accurately.

Hamilton and Shinn (2003) documented that teachers often believe their students have reading comprehension problems when, in fact, they are weak in component skills of word recognition and automatic reading of words.

Most students on the bottom 40 percent of the achievement continuum will benefit from careful and deliberate instruction in the full range of component skills because their reading problems are attributable to a combination of the problems described above. Strands of a good intervention program may include or emphasize phonological, orthographic, morphological, semantic, and syntactic language processes (Berninger & Richards, 2002; Carreker, 2005; Greene, 2008). Wolf's (2003) *RAVE-O* program, for example, includes strands that teach automatic word recognition, automatic recognition of rime chunks, vocabulary elaboration (through multiple-meaning words), and decodable text reading. *RAVE-O* was developed to help very poor readers (Tier 3) in grades 2–3.

Students With Phonologically Based Reading Difficulties

Students with phonological weaknesses are, by definition, inaccurate on phonic word attack (i.e., nonsense-word reading and real-word reading). This is true for older, poor readers as well as young readers. To make progress, intermediate-level students must often relearn and practice the basics before they can move ahead. Skills they usually need include letter formation, symbol-sound/sound-symbol connections, recognition of syllables and morphemes, word reading, spelling, and reading aloud with sufficient fluency.

In the initial stages of developing accuracy in letter-sound associations, cues—such as pictures, objects, gestures, and key words—may be used. In the later stages, cues are dropped. Cues may be necessary for vowels long after they are necessary for consonants. Multisensory-association techniques are especially important for students who struggle with letter-sound associations. One effective practice is presenting selected letters and spellings on cards and having students respond with the correct letter sounds. Another practice has the teacher say phonemes and then ask students to select or write the graphemes that correspond to the phonemes.

Teachers may want to establish fairly rigorous standards for accuracy when setting reading goals for students. There is some evidence that a 98 percent accuracy level at third grade is a better predictor of student performance on high-stakes reading comprehension measures than WCPM (Davidson, Allen, & Farrell, 2008).

Dysfluent Poor Readers: Can We Speed Them Up?

After students have developed automaticity with single syllables or words, units can be combined into two-syllable or compound words. For example, students can be given sets of words containing contrasting spelling patterns, such as closed vs. silent-**e** syllables (e.g., **can** vs. **cane**):

- First, students look at the print and mark the vowels as long or short.
- Then, students go back and read the words aloud.
- Students can also be asked to scan a page of words or syllables and locate those with a specific characteristic, such as a vowel combination.

Whatever the specific strategy, the purpose is to focus the student's attention on the print, the sounds, and the connections between them. For variety, students can read words by saying the vowel sound first. After the patterns have been marked and practiced, students are then timed on reading the set of words to establish a baseline. Then the set is practiced until mastered.

Some students remain slow readers in spite of much practice. The later we identify students who are struggling with basic reading skills, the more likely it is they will remain slow readers. Torgesen and his colleagues (2001) have shown that students whose remediation begins in third grade or beyond are far less likely to achieve satisfactory reading fluency than students who are identified and helped in first grade. Other researchers, including Meyer and Felton (1999), Wolf and Katzir-Cohen (2001), and Fuchs et al. (2001), have shown that students with the most intractable reading problems almost always remain significantly slower than their age-mates. Again, labored, inaccurate reading leads to comparatively little reading practice because the student cannot sustain the effort of prolonged oral or silent reading. In turn, the lack of practice is associated with diminished vocabulary and declining language comprehension in relation to age-mates.

Some students with dysfluency have not had enough practice applying skills that are basically intact; they have adequate phonological skills and can sound out words reasonably well (ELLs may fall into this category). Their problems should be less severe and easier to correct than those of students with phonologically based decoding problems. Motivation and instruction often play a role with this type of student. They need concentrated oral-language instruction and many hours of guided oral-reading practice with the techniques described in this module.

> ### Activity for Increasing Word-Reading Speed: "Land the Fish" Game
> (This game is used in *The Herman Reading Method*™
> [Herman, in revision] for intermediate, Tier 3 readers working in groups of three.)
>
> To develop fluency in word reading, teach students who are working in a small group to play "Land the Fish." In this game, use word cards of only words that students have been taught to read and that they can read with accuracy. The object of the game is for each student to land as many fish (e.g., word cards) as possible.
>
> - Shuffle about 16 word cards and place them in a stack facedown in the center of a table.
> - Players take turns, starting with the student to the left of the teacher.
> - The first player picks up the top word card from the stack and thereby "catches" a fish.
> - To "land" the fish, the player must read the word on the card *in 3 seconds or less*. (The teacher counts to three silently to establish the 3-second time span.)
> - If the player is able to read the word correctly in the time allotted, he lands the fish and puts the card facedown in front of him. Then, the next player has a turn.
> - If a player is unable to read the word in the time allotted, he places the word card at the bottom of the card pile in the center of the table and the next player has a turn.
> - The game is over when all of the fish have been landed.

Phrase-Cued Oral Reading   *from Florida Center already marked...*

Phrases are groups of words that cluster together as meaningful chunks of sentences. The phrasing that characterizes the prosody, or intonation, of good readers can be modeled and taught directly. Phrasing is the result of sentence comprehension; understanding a sentence's meaning leads to grouping of words into phrases.

Phrase-Cued Oral Reading Procedure

1. Explain to students that grouping words together into phrases will help them with fluency and comprehension. Then model reading the phrases of your choice, which

may be written on sentence strips or listed on an overhead transparency or white board. Some phrase suggestions:

up the tree	if you can
why we are going	all around town
when he asked	could have been
in back of the house	away from everyone
more and more	not on your life

2. Put sentence text that includes the phrases on an overhead projector or white board, or use a text copy that you can write on. Provide one copy of the text that the student can read from.

3. Mark up the sentence(s) into phrases, using a dot or slash mark after each phrase:

Alice / fell way down / into the rabbit hole. /

Alice / was beginning / to get very tired / of sitting / by her sister / on the bank, / and of having nothing / to do /.

4. Using the eraser end of a pencil (or a marker on the transparency), scoop under the phrases as the student reads the sentence(s) aloud.

5. Then, have the student read the sentence(s) again, scooping under the phrases with his own pencil eraser.

Exercise 3.2 Practice Phrase-Cued Oral Reading and View a Video Demonstration

- Find a partner. Select a passage from *Alice's Adventures in Wonderland*. Mark the phrases with slashes or dots.
- Take turns with the Teacher role, modeling reading of the phrases. Scoop under the phrases with a pencil eraser as you read.

Video Demonstration
(*Teaching Reading Essentials* [Moats & Farrell, 2007], Part 3, Demonstration 21)

- Watch the video, then answer this question.

    — How does the teacher explain the activity?

    _____

    _____

Simultaneous Oral Reading (SOR)

In older reading textbooks, SOR was also called the "neurological-impress method" (Heckelman, 1969). This method, designed to support students who lack fluency and confidence, is used one-on-one. The brain *does* respond to novel practice! The teacher or coach reads simultaneously with, or slightly ahead of, the student, modeling good phrasing and providing a sense of fluent reading as his voice pulls the student along.

SOR Procedure

1. Select a short story or passage that the student can read accurately (i.e., no more than one error for every 10–15 words).
2. Before launching into the SOR exercise, preview the story by discussing the topic, illustrations, or titles with the student. Preview any challenging vocabulary that the student will encounter. Explain that you two will try to read a section with one voice.
3. Using good expression, read a portion of the story/passage aloud while the student looks at the words being read and follows the text with her finger or a pencil eraser.
4. The adult and the student read the text segment aloud together, trying to read with one voice. Track the text with your finger, leading the student along.
    *   This step may be repeated two or three times until the student is ready to read the selection independently. The student may also be encouraged to practice reading the text silently.
    *   The student reads aloud to the adult, and the adult helps the student record her time and errors on a simple graph.

[handwritten note: read it like your telling a story → read faster but smoothly...]

Exercise 3.3	**View a Video Demonstration and Role-Play SOR**

(*Teaching Reading Essentials* [Moats & Farrell, 2007], Part 3, Demonstration 23)

*   Watch the video, then answer these questions.

    1. What two techniques does the teacher use to make certain the student knows the words in the upcoming text?

        _____

        _____

    2. Does the teacher model and give strategies for increasing speed? Where and how?

        _____

        _____

(continued)

Exercise 3.3 (continued)

SOR Role-Play

- Practice simultaneous oral reading with a partner. Sitting next to each other, decide who will be the teacher and who will be the student.

- Using a text you have already read or previewed, such as *Alice's Adventures in Wonderland*, practice the five-step SOR procedure just described. The teacher models and leads the student.

Reread-Adapt and Answer-Comprehend (RAAC) Intervention

Developed by Therrien, Gormley, and Kubina (2006), RAAC is a structured approach to the repeated reading technique described earlier in this chapter. RAAC was shown to be effective with students who have both fluency and text comprehension problems and who read between first- and third-grade levels. Before implementation, the teacher must select a target performance criterion in relation to established norms and students' baseline reading fluency levels. Appropriate reading material should be selected. Passages should be short and focused on one complete idea. The suggested passage length by grade is as follows:

- Grade 1: 53–66 words
- Grade 2: 89–111 words
- Grade 3: 107–133 words
- Grade 4: 123–153 words

RAAC Procedure

1. Prompt the student:
   - "Read as quickly and as carefully as you can. Pay attention to what you are reading, as you will need to answer a few questions when you finish."
   - Ask the student to respond to question-generation prompts (i.e., Who . . . ?; What . . . ?; When . . . ?; Where . . . ?; Why . . . ?; How . . . ?).
2. Have the student reread to a partner or into tape recorder until she reaches her goal.
3. Have the student read for you, correcting errors and providing feedback.
4. Praise the student and/or reward her with a sticker or points.
5. *Adapt and answer:* Have the student answer questions you have placed on cue cards.
6. *End and adjust:* If, in three consecutive sessions, the student is not able to reach her fluency goal, lower the reading material by one grade level. If the student reaches her goal in two or fewer readings in three sessions, raise the level of reading material by one grade level.

A similar approach was very effective in improving the reading comprehension of older students in grades 4–8 (Therrien, Wickstrom, & Jones, 2006; see abstract, following). Note that the emphasis is on *reading for meaning*!

(Therrien, Wickstrom, & Jones, 2006)

Abstract: Research was conducted to ascertain if a combined repeated reading and question generation intervention was effective at improving the reading achievement of fourth through eighth grade students with learning disabilities or who were at risk for reading failure. Students were assigned to a treatment or control group via a stratified random sampling. Instructional components and training were based on best practices reported in the literature. Students receiving intervention significantly improved their reading speed and ability to answer inferential comprehension questions on passages that were reread. Compared to the control group, students in the intervention group also made significant gains in oral reading fluency on independent passages.

Reader's Theatre: A Fun (but less effective) Practice

Reader's Theatre (Tyler & Chard, 2000; Worthy & Prater, 2002) is a highly motivating, engaging, and enjoyable classroom activity. Historical, dramatic, and poetic texts are selected for theatrical readings. The texts are parsed into segments that are assigned to specific students, who then read and virtually memorize their passage until they read it in the sequence of the dramatic dialogue. The performance aspect of Reader's Theatre is entertaining, engaging, and adaptable to many kinds and levels of text.

If the goal of an intervention is fluency-building, however, the teacher must be careful to measure the effect and benefit of Reader's Theatre activities for the specific students they are designed to help. Students may memorize their parts without getting much reading practice and/or may not get the benefit of direct feedback about their own reading rate. This activity may not provide the amount of direct, structured practice that at-risk students need to close the reading gap with their peers.

Students' response to instruction and remediation is often the only way to be sure who is constitutionally afflicted with a biological limitation of reading skill (i.e., a learning disability) and who is very teachable. In Chapter 4, we turn our attention to fluency measurement and progress-monitoring, which are essential tools for preventing and ameliorating persistent reading problems, regardless of their nature.

Review: Evaluate Fluency in Your Reading Program

- Survey the teacher's manual from your core, comprehensive reading program to evaluate the use of fluency-building activities and methods.

1. Which of the skill-building activities described in Chapter 2 are integral and regular parts of the program you are using?

_____

_____

_____

_____

_____

2. Which of the activities for building text-reading fluency described in Chapter 3 are integral and regular parts of the program you are using?

_____

_____

_____

_____

_____

3. If you were to supplement your program, especially for struggling readers, which additional activities or methods would you be likely to use? For whom? Why?

_____

_____

_____

_____

_____

Chapter 4 — The Measurement of Reading Fluency

Learner Objectives for Chapter 4

- Understand the use of oral reading fluency (ORF) as an assessment tool for screening and monitoring progress.
- Learn the importance of charting progress and using data to inform instructional decisions.

Warm-Up: Observe ORF

(Video from DIBELS® [Good & Kaminski, 2002])

- View a video of the administration of an ORF assessment.
  - Can you tell if the student was reading fluently, just by listening?

  _____

  _____

  _____

  - What enables someone to be a fluent reader?

  _____

  _____

  _____

  - Can listening to a person read provide valid and reliable assessment information about reading proficiency?

  _____

  _____

  _____

The History and Definition of Curriculum-Based Measurement (CBM)

Oral reading fluency is both a desirable quality of reading and a measurable indicator of overall reading proficiency. We teach students to become fluent readers using techniques reviewed in previous chapters of this module, and we can measure students' proficiency in reading by administering fluency assessments.

The measures most often used to screen and monitor progress on reading proficiency are known as curriculum-based measures (CBMs). These measures were developed more than 30 years ago at the University of Minnesota by Stan Deno (1985) and colleagues (Fuchs & Deno, 1991; Hosp & Fuchs, 2005; Hosp, Hosp, & Howell, 2007; Shinn, 1998). CBMs are drawn from a family of measures called general outcome measures (GOMs), which sample content that students should have mastered by the end of the grade level that the measure represents.

CBMs are used at the beginning of the school year in September, when students are screened in relation to a goal they should achieve by the end of the school year. In addition, student progress is monitored with CBMs, which allow teachers to determine whether skills are being acquired at an adequate pace or rate so that targeted goals can be met by the end of the school year.

Mastery measures differ from CBMs (see *Table 4.1*). Teachers use mastery measures—weekly tests, unit tests, or theme tests—to assess when a student has mastered what was taught over a shorter time span rather than to assess student progress toward a predetermined annual goal.

Table 4.1. Differences Between Mastery Measures and CBMs

Mastery Measures	CBMs
Focus on specific skills taught during the school year	Measure what should be known by the end of the school year
Are administered after a unit or sequence of lessons designed to promote mastery	Are used for monitoring progress toward that end-of-year goal
Are informal and not standardized	Are standardized, reliable, and valid
Allow scaffolds, supports, and adjustments	Require standard administration and scoring

CBMs require students to perform tasks that are similar to those they would be expected to perform in a classroom (e.g., reading aloud is a component of classroom instruction). As discussed in Chapter 1 of this module, reading aloud (ORF) provides a teacher with important information about a student's overall reading skill. CBMs, including ORF, include the following characteristics:

- The results are reliable and valid (unlike many informal measures).

- The tasks are standardized and include reading aloud from equivalent passages and/ or selecting missing words in maze passages (i.e., passages with every seventh word deleted).
- The stimulus materials may be drawn from instructional materials, but only if their difficulty is calibrated to match other standardized grade-level passages.
- There are specific requirements for administration, student directions, and scoring procedures. This level of standardization is required to ensure reliability and validity of the data for both individual students and groups of students. These standards also allow for the development of local norms.
- The scores are obtained by counting the correct and incorrect responses in a specified time period. The ORF measure requires a student to read from a passage for 1 minute, and the score is the number of words read correctly in that time period.
- Performance is repeatedly sampled across time. Students respond to different but equivalent stimulus materials drawn from the same general source. For example, the DIBELS® (Good & Kaminski, 2002) Oral Reading Fluency measure includes three passages for screening and 20 equivalent passages for monitoring progress.
- They are efficient and typically take 1–3 minutes to administer.
- They are easy to teach and to learn so that a variety of professionals, paraprofessionals, and parents can learn the procedures.

The graph in *Figure 4.1* illustrates the progress of a fourth grade student who has undergone 6 weeks of intervention. Note the recording of WCPM and the number of mistakes.

Figure 4.1. A Sample CBM Progress Graph

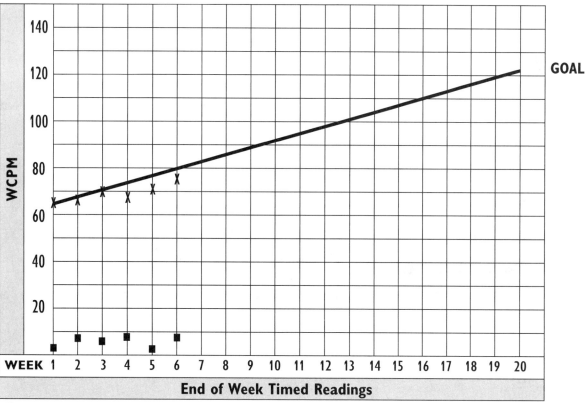

Time = X   Errors = ■

Advantages of CBMs

Teachers can use CBM data to:

- Improve instructional programs for individual students. *Figure 4.1* illustrates how a teacher can set goals, monitor progress, and gauge the efficacy of an intervention, modifying it when necessary according to the data.
- Predict student performance on high-stakes tests and be assured that the student scores are valid and reliable indicators of reading proficiency.
- Set reasonable and ambitious goals for students. Having specific targets for learning has been shown to improve student progress because teachers who set tangible goals tend to make more timely and appropriate instructional changes based on progress-monitoring data (Fuchs et al., 1993).
- Graph student progress, providing a powerful visual display for students and parents. The clarity of the information can enhance communication and provide students with a much better understanding of their own goals and progress.
- Formulate Response to Intervention (RtI) as both screening and progress-monitoring measures. These data can also be used to evaluate a Tier 2 or Tier 3 intervention to determine whether it is of sufficient intensity and duration for the student to meet the intended goal.

Recording ORF Scores

These rules for scoring ORF in a standardized way are recommended by Hasbrouck and Tindal (2006). Students read aloud from *unpracticed* text at either their instructional level or their goal level. An error includes any word that is:

- omitted;
- mispronounced;
- substituted; or
- transposed in a phrase.

If a word is read incorrectly more than once, it counts as an error each time. Not counted as errors are words that are read correctly and repeated more than once, errors that are self-corrected by the student, and words that are mispronounced due to dialect or speech impairments. A word inserted that does not appear in the text is not counted as an error because the final score is an indication of the number of words that are read correctly in the text.

Exercise 4.1   Score an ORF Assessment

- Keep score as your presenter, playing the role of a struggling reader, reads one of the following passages aloud for 1 minute.

(continued)

Exercise 4.1 (continued)

DIBELS® (6th ed.) Grade 1 Oral Reading Fluency Passage
ORF Scoring Practice Passage
(from Good & Kaminski, 2002)

My Soccer Team

I am so happy! I just found out I can be on the soccer team.	15
We have our first practice on Saturday. We practice at my school	27
right after lunch.	30
Our team is called the Blue Bombers. Our colors are blue and	42
white so I get to wear blue shorts and a blue and white shirt. The	57
number on my shirt is seven. I'm seven years old, too. I think	70
seven must be my lucky number.	76
We play our first game next week on Saturday. I can't wait	88
to play. My dad said if I practice a lot I will do well at the games.	105
My dad is going to practice with me tonight.	114
Right after dinner my dad is going to take me to the store to	128
buy some soccer shoes and a soccer ball. Then we will play on	141
the grass by my school. My dad will help me to kick the ball and	156
to run fast and kick the ball at the same time.	167
I am so excited I don't think I will get to sleep tonight. But I	182
better sleep so that I can be rested and strong for my soccer	195
practice.	196

WCPM: Count the number of words read correctly during
the 1-minute period.

Total words: _____ – errors: _____ = WCPM: _____

(continued)

Exercise 4.1 (continued)

DIBELS® (6th ed.) Grade 6 Benchmark 1.1
ORF Scoring Practice Passage
(from Good & Kaminski, 2002)

The Grand Canyon

What is one of the world's biggest holes in the ground? It's	12
more than a mile deep and almost three hundred miles long, and	24
more than ten miles wide at some points. If you guessed the	36
Grand Canyon, you're right. The Grand Canyon is an enormous	46
gorge carved over millions of years by the Colorado River in	57
northwestern Arizona.	59
Among the world's great tourist attractions, the Grand	67
Canyon is walled by colorful strata, or layers, of rock dating	78
back millions of years. The reds, pinks, and yellows in the rock	90
are the result of traces of different minerals.	98
Most tourists visit the South Rim of the canyon, where there	109
are hotels and many trails to explore. Bright Angel Trail is a	121
popular hiking trail. The South Rim is open year round to	132
visitors. The North Rim is cooler and quieter than the South Rim	144
but is open only six months of the year.	153
The only ways to reach the inner canyon are by foot, on	165
mule, or by raft on the Colorado River. Visitors can take daylong	177
raft trips over smooth water or weeklong trips that include	187
rolling rapids. Almost two hundred years ago, American John	196
Wesley Powell led the first successful trip through the canyon.	206
He and ten other men traveled down the river in four small boats,	219
braving waters that had never been mapped.	226
Native Americans were the first to live and work in the	237
canyon, more than eight hundred years ago. They lived in rock	248
pueblos on both rims of the canyon, hunting and fishing,	258
growing crops, making pottery, and weaving baskets.	265

(continued)

Exercise 4.1   (continued)

The Grand Canyon (continued)

Wildlife is abundant in the canyon. Hundreds of kinds of	275
birds live there, as well as bighorn sheep, mule deer, beavers,	286
bats, snakes, lizards, and frogs. There are also many types of	297
trees, cacti, and wildflowers.	301
You can see that the Grand Canyon is much more than just a	314
big hole in the ground. It is an amazing site, alive with stories of	328
the past and present that are written on the rock, on the land, and	342
on the river.	345

WCPM: Count the number of words read correctly during
the 1-minute period.

Total words: _____ – errors: _____ = WCPM: _____

Calculating ORF Percent Accuracy and WCPM

With the advent of hand-held scoring devices, published assessments, and computer-generated fluency charts, teachers seldom need to calculate fluency themselves. But just in case no such aid is available (heaven forbid!), let's review the simple formulas that yield percent accuracy and WCPM:

$$\text{Percent accuracy} = \frac{\text{\# of words read correctly}}{\text{total number of words read}}$$

$$\text{Fluency (WCPM)} = \frac{\text{\# of words read correctly}}{\text{total reading time}}$$

1. Count the number of words read correctly by subtracting errors from total words read.
2. Calculate percent accuracy by dividing total words read correctly by total words read. (The percent value will indicate whether the passage was within the student's instructional reading level ability.)
3. Convert the number of seconds of the reading to a decimal (i.e., proportion of a minute) by dividing the number of seconds by 60.
4. Calculate WCPM by dividing the number of words read correctly by the total reading time in decimal form.

Example:
- A student read a story with 120 words in 2 minutes, 40 seconds (160 seconds).
- She made 25 errors.
  1. Number of words read correctly = (120 − 25) = 95
  2. Percent accuracy = 95 ÷ 120 = 79 percent
  3. Total time in decimal form = 160 ÷ 60 = 2.67 minutes
  4. WCPM = 95 ÷ 2.67 = 36 WCPM

Note that the example student was reading a passage that was too difficult for her. (Instructional level passages should be read with 90–95 percent accuracy.) For universal screening purposes, students should be administered passages at their grade level. However, for monitoring progress during a Tier 2 or Tier 3 intervention, passages should be at the student's instructional level.

Exercise 4.2	**Practice Calculating ORF Percent Accuracy and WCPM**

- A student read a third grade passage for 1 minute.
- She read 53 words correctly, and she made 7 errors.

1. Is the student reading at or near the 50th percentile for third grade?

   _____

2. What percentage of words did she read accurately?

   _____

3. How would you summarize this score? Is the student not at risk, at some risk, or at significant risk based on this score?

   _____

What if Students Are Far Below Grade Level?

Although progress monitoring is usually done with grade-level passages, students with serious reading difficulties who are far below grade level should read from text that is one or two levels below the desired goal. Since they must read from unpracticed text, it should be within a difficulty level they can handle, defined as a 90 percent or better success rate.

Charting Fluency Data

Students who get involved in charting their own data will be much more motivated to work at improving their scores from assessment to assessment. Charts should be designed to show small increments of gain that will become significant over time. Charts should track both fluency data (which should gradually increase) and error rates (which should stay low). If the number of errors is too high, the student's instruction should emphasize reteaching and accuracy before any emphasis on fluency is appropriate. Be sure to mark the goal toward which the student is working; keep the expectations reasonable, but keep them high!

Exercise 4.3 | Chart Progress-Monitoring WCPM Data

- Given the following data, enter the scores on the chart on the next page. The first data point is the benchmark score.

> ### 65 WCPM, 6 errors (benchmark median scores)
>
> This student is beginning grade 3. Duration of the small-group instruction is 12 weeks.

— What is an appropriate aim line, or goal line? Mark that line on the chart.

— Now, enter the following progress-monitoring data on the chart:

> Week 2: . . . . . .67 WCPM, 4 errors
>
> Week 3: . . . . . .70 WCPM, 5 errors
>
> Week 4: . . . . . .75 WCPM, 6 errors
>
> Week 5: . . . . . .69 WCPM, 6 errors
>
> Week 6: . . . . . .76 WCPM, 5 errors
>
> Week 7: . . . . . .78 WCPM, 7 errors
>
> Week 8: . . . . . .80 WCPM, 4 errors
>
> Week 9: . . . . . .77 WCPM, 6 errors
>
> Week 10: . . . . .82 WCPM, 7 errors

— Given the trend in these data, does it look as if the instruction is appropriate (i.e., is the student responding to the intervention)?

_____

— Is the text that is being used for timed readings at the right level of difficulty for this student?

_____

(continued)

Exercise 4.3 (continued)

CBM Progress Graph

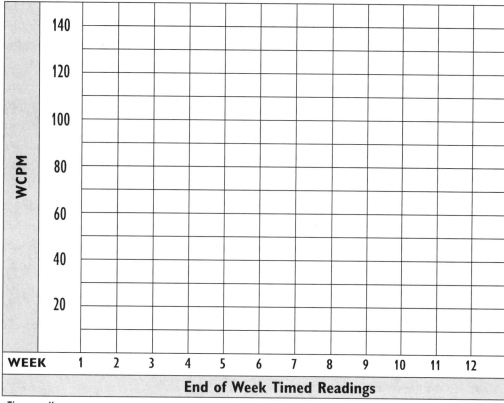

Time = X   Errors = ■

Summary

As with any complex skill, reading fluency develops as a consequence of extensive practice with a set of subskills and the integration of those skills in the service of purposeful reading. Before students can be automatic at word recognition, they must be accurate. To be accurate, they need to know letters, sounds, decoding strategies, and vocabulary meanings. If those skills are strong, students are more likely to recognize a large number of words without having to sound them out. Students have automatic word-reading skills when the mind effortlessly and accurately connects print with speech.

Fluency is the achievement of adequate reading speed to support text comprehension. Reading print with automaticity gives the mind more "desk space" to devote to comprehension. Listening to a good reader, one can tell that the reader understands what he is reading because his phrasing, emphasis, and voice contour convey the meaning of the language. Students who are fluent are more likely to be avid readers outside of school and to experience the benefit of substantial text exposure.

Simple measures of reading fluency—both of critical subskills and text-reading itself—are among the best screening, progress-monitoring, and outcome measures available to the field. If students are not fluent text readers, it is highly likely that their overall reading achievement, as measured on summative tests of silent passage-reading, will be inadequate to sustain grade-level performance. Fluency-based measurement of reading skill is efficient, accurate, and valid.

When students lack sufficient fluency, the cause may be lack of basic or advanced decoding skill, lack of automatic processing capabilities, unfamiliarity with English, or insufficient reading practice. Diagnostic tests are sometimes needed to determine the cause of dysfluent reading before an intervention plan can be designed.

Most students develop fluency as a consequence of good basic skills, guided oral-reading practice, and independent reading at the right level of difficulty. Slow readers with persistent fluency problems respond to several types of validated interventions. The poorest readers, at Tiers 2 and 3, need continuing instruction in the basics as well as text-reading practice. Students who have mastered the basics yet still struggle, including those with weak language comprehension, need more emphasis on techniques such as partner-reading, repeated readings, and simultaneous oral reading. Not all fluency problems stem from the same cause or respond to the same treatment.

Finally, not all students need deliberate work on reading fluency. Those who will benefit should be identified with a validated, reliable screening tool. The goal of intervention is never to "read faster"; it is to read smoothly, with comprehension, and a sense of enjoyment. The goal is to experience the intrinsic rewards of access to written language.

Take 2 Review

- Return to the definition of *reading fluency* that you wrote at the beginning of Chapter 1. Rewrite that definition with any changes you would like to make.

_____

_____

_____

_____

- At the end of Chapter 1, you posed three questions that you wanted to have answered as you studied this module. Were those questions addressed or are they still unanswered? Write what you have learned about the answers to your questions.

Question 1: _____

_____

_____

_____

_____

Question 2: _____

_____

_____

_____

_____

Question 3: _____

_____

_____

_____

_____

Final Quiz, Module 5

1. In what ways are reading fluency and reading comprehension related?

    _____
    _____
    _____
    _____
    _____
    _____

2. How would you know if a student has adequate reading fluency for her age and grade level?

    _____
    _____
    _____
    _____
    _____
    _____

3. What approaches to enhancement of reading fluency are supported by research?

    _____
    _____
    _____
    _____
    _____
    _____

4. For what type of student would it be *inappropriate* to conduct repeated readings on timed reading passages?

    _____
    _____
    _____
    _____
    _____
    _____

Glossary

affix: a morpheme or a meaningful part of a word that is attached before or after a root to modify its meaning; a category that includes prefixes, suffixes, and infixes

alphabetic principle: the principle that letters are used to represent individual phonemes in the spoken word; a critical insight for beginning reading and spelling

alphabetic writing system: a system of symbols that represent each consonant and vowel sound in a language

automaticity: when a learned skill can be performed without conscious attention

base word: a free morpheme, usually of Anglo-Saxon origin, to which affixes can be added

chunk: a group of letters, processed as a unit, that corresponds to a piece of a word, usually a consonant cluster, rime pattern, syllable, or morpheme

concept: an idea that links other facts, words, and ideas together into a coherent whole

consonant: a phoneme (speech sound) that is not a vowel and that is formed by obstructing the flow of air with the teeth, lips, or tongue; also called a *closed sound* in some instructional programs; English has 25 consonant phonemes

context: the language that surrounds a given word or phrase (linguistic context), or the field of meaningful associations that surrounds a given word or phrase (experiential context)

context processor: the neural networks that bring background knowledge and discourse to bear as word meanings are processed

cumulative instruction: teaching that proceeds in additive steps, building on what was previously taught

decodable text: text in which a high proportion (i.e., 70–90 percent) of words comprise sound-symbol relationships that have already been taught; used to provide practice with specific decoding skills; a bridge between learning phonics and the application of phonics in independent reading of text

decoding: the ability to translate a word from print to speech, usually by employing knowledge of sound-symbol correspondences; also the act of deciphering a new word by sounding it out

derivational suffix: a type of bound morpheme; a suffix—such as **-ity**, **-ive**, and **-ly**—that can change the part of speech of the root or base word to which it is added

direct instruction: instruction in which the teacher defines and teaches a concept, guides students through its application, and arranges extended guided practice for students until mastery is achieved

discourse structure: organizational conventions in longer segments of oral or written language

double deficit: an impairment of both phonological processing and speed of naming sequential arrays of letters, numbers, objects, and/or colors

dyslexia: an impairment of reading accuracy and fluency attributable to an underlying phonological deficit

fluency: in reading, to read with sufficient speed to support understanding

grapheme: a letter or letter combination that spells a phoneme; can be one, two, three, or four letters in English (e.g., **e**, **ei**, **igh**, **eigh**)

inflection: a type of bound morpheme; a grammatical ending that does not change the part of speech of a word but that marks its tense, number, or degree in English (e.g., **-s**, **-ed**, **-ing**)

integrated: lesson components that are interwoven and flow smoothly together

lexicon: the name for the mental dictionary in every person's linguistic processing system

longitudinal: a type of study that selects and then follows subjects over a long period of time

long-term memory: the memory system that stores information beyond 24 hours

meaning processor: the neural networks that attach meanings to words that have been heard or decoded

metalinguistic awareness: an acquired level of awareness of language structure and function that allows us to reflect on and consciously manipulate the language we use

morpheme: the smallest meaningful unit of a language; it may be a word or part of a word; it may be one or more syllables (e.g., **un-inter-rupt-ible**)

morphology: the study of the meaningful units in a language and how they are combined in word formation

morphophonemic: having to do with both sound and meaning

multisyllabic: having more than one syllable

naming speed: timed performance on a test of naming letters, numbers, colors, objects; see also *rapid automatic naming*

NRP: Initialism for the Report of the National Reading Panel (National Institute of Child Health and Human Development, 2000)

onset-rime: the natural division of a syllable into two parts, the onset coming before the vowel and the rime including the vowel and what follows it (e.g., **pl–an, shr–ill**)

orthographic processor: the neural networks responsible for perceiving, storing, and retrieving letter sequences in words

orthography: a writing system for representing language

phoneme: a speech sound that combines with others in a language system to make words; English has 40 to 44 phonemes, according to various linguists

phoneme awareness (also, **phonemic awareness**): the conscious awareness that words are made up of segments of our own speech that are represented with letters in an alphabetic orthography

phonics: the study of the relationships between letters and the sounds they represent; also used as a descriptor for code-based instruction in reading (i.e., "the phonics approach" or "phonic reading")

phonological awareness: metalinguistic awareness of all levels of the speech sound system, including word boundaries, stress patterns, syllables, onset-rime units, and phonemes; a more encompassing term than *phoneme awareness*

phonological processor: a neural network in the frontal and temporal areas of the brain, usually the left cerebral hemisphere, that is specialized for speech-sound perception, memory, retrieval, and pronunciation

phonological working memory: the "online" memory system that remembers speech long enough to extract meaning from it, or that holds onto words during writing; a function of the phonological processor

phonology: the rule system within a language by which phonemes can be sequenced, combined, and pronounced to make words

pragmatics: the system of rules and conventions for using language and related gestures in a social context

prefix: a morpheme that precedes a root and that contributes to or modifies the meaning of a word; a common linguistic unit in Latin-based words

prosody: the rhythmic and intonational aspect of spoken language

rapid automatic naming (RAN) (also referred to as *rapid serial naming* [RSN]): the act of naming rows of limited sets of repeating colors, objects, letters, and numbers; also, a specific test developed by Denckla and Rudel (1976)

reading fluency: the speed and accuracy of oral reading; the ability to read text with sufficient speed to support comprehension

root: a bound morpheme, usually of Latin origin, that cannot stand alone but that is used to form a family of words with related meanings

semantics: the study of word and phrase meanings and relationships

sound–symbol correspondence (same as *phoneme-grapheme correspondence*): the rules and patterns by which letters and letter combinations represent speech sounds

suffix: a derivational morpheme (added to a root or base word) that often changes the word's part of speech and modifies its meaning

syllable: the unit of pronunciation that is organized around a vowel; it may or may not have consonants before or after the vowel

syntax: the system of rules governing permissible word order in sentences

vowel: one of a set of 15 vowel phonemes in English, not including vowel-**r** combinations; an open phoneme that is the nucleus of every syllable; classified by tongue position and height (e.g., high to low, front to back)

word recognition: the instant recognition of a whole word in print

References

Adams, G. N., & Brown, S. (2007a). *The six-minute solution: A reading fluency program (intermediate level)*. Longmont, CO: Sopris West Educational Services.

Adams, G. N., & Brown, S. (2007b). *The six-minute solution: A reading fluency program (primary level)*. Longmont, CO: Sopris West Educational Services.

Adams, G. N., & Brown, S. (2007c). *The six-minute solution: A reading fluency program (secondary level)*. Longmont, CO: Sopris West Educational Services.

Arguelles, M., & Baker, S. (in press). *Teaching English language learners: A supplementary LETRS® module*. Longmont, CO: Sopris West Educational Services.

Beck, R., Anderson, P., & Conrad, D. (2008). *Practicing basic skills in reading: One-minute fluency builders series*. Longmont, CO: Sopris West Educational Services.

Beck, R., & Clement, R. (1991). The Great Falls precision teaching project: A historical review. *Journal of Precision Teaching, 8*(2), 8–12.

Berninger, V., & Richards, T. (2002). *Brain literacy for educators and psychologists*. New York: Academic Press.

Carreker, S. (2005). Teaching reading: Accurate decoding and fluency. In J. Birsh (Ed.), *Multisensory teaching of basic language skills* (2nd ed.) (pp. 213–255). Baltimore: Paul H. Brookes.

Carroll, L. (1866). *Alice's adventures in wonderland*. London: Macmillan.

Chall, J. (1996). *Stages of reading development* (2nd ed.). Orlando, FL: Harcourt Brace.

Chard, D., Vaughn, S., & Tyler, B. (2002). A synthesis of research on effective interventions for building fluency with elementary students with learning disabilities. *Journal of Learning Disabilities, 35*, 386–406.

Connor, C. M., Morrison, F. J., & Katch, L. E. (2004). Beyond the reading wars: Exploring the effect of child-instruction interactions on growth in early reading. *Scientific Studies of Reading, 8*, 305–336.

Cunningham, A., & Stanovich, K. (1991). Tracking the unique effects of print exposure in children: Associations with vocabulary, general knowledge, and spelling. *Journal of Educational Psychology, 83*(2), 264–274.

Cunningham, A. E., & Stanovich, K. E. (1998). What reading does for the mind. *American Educator, 22*(1 & 2), 8–15.

Davidson, M., Allen, D., & Farrell, L. (2008). *The role of accuracy in reading rate and accuracy measures*. Manuscript submitted for publication.

Denckla, M., & Rudel, R. (1976). *Rapid automatic naming test* (RAN). Austin, TX: Pro-Ed.

Deno, S. L. (1985). Curriculum-based measurement: The emerging alternative. *Exceptional Children, 52*, 219–232.

Dodson, J. (2008). *50 nifty activities for 5 components and 3 tiers of reading instruction*. Longmont, CO: Sopris West Educational Services.

Ebbers, S. (2007). *Power readers*. Longmont, CO: Sopris West Educational Services.

Ehri, L. C. (2004). Teaching phonemic awareness and phonics: An explanation of the National Reading Panel meta-analysis. In P. McCardle & V. Chhabra (Eds.), *The voice of evidence in reading research* (pp. 153–186). Baltimore: Paul H. Brookes.

Ehri, L. C. (1997). Sight word learning in normal readers and dyslexics. In B. Blachman (Ed.), *Foundations of reading acquisition and dyslexia* (pp. 163–189). Mahwah, NJ: Lawrence Erlbaum.

Ehri, L. C. (1996). Development of the ability to read words. In R. Barr, M. Kamil, P. B. Mosenthal, & P. D. Pearson (Eds.), *Handbook of reading research: Vol. II* (pp. 383–418). Mahwah, NJ: Lawrence Erlbaum.

Ehri, L. C., & Snowling, M. J. (2004). Developmental variation in word recognition. In A. C. Stone, E. R. Silliman, B. J. Ehren, & K. Apel (Eds.), *Handbook of language and literacy: Development and disorders* (pp. 443–460). New York: Guilford Press.

Fletcher, J., Lyon, G. R., Fuchs, L., & Barnes, M. A. (2007). *Learning disabilities: From identification to intervention*. New York: Guilford Press.

Fuchs, L. S., & Deno, S. L. (1991). Curriculum-based measurement: Current applications and future directions. *Exceptional Children, 57,* 466–501.

Fuchs, L. S., Fuchs, D., Hamlett, C. L., Walz, L., & Germann, G. (1993). Formative evaluation of academic progress: How much growth should we expect? *School Psychology Review, 22,* 27–48.

Fuchs, L. S., Fuchs, D., Hosp, M. K., & Jenkins, J. (2001). Oral reading fluency as an indicator of reading competence: A theoretical, empirical & historical analysis. *Scientific Studies of Reading, 5*(3), 239–256.

Glaser, D. (2005). *ParaReading: A training guide for tutors*. Longmont, CO: Sopris West Educational Services.

Glaser, D., & Moats, L. C. (2008). LETRS® *Foundations: An introduction to language and literacy*. Longmont, CO: Sopris West Educational Services.

Good, R. H., III, & Kaminski, R. A. (Eds.). (2002). *Dynamic Indicators of Basic Early Literacy Skills* (DIBELS®) (6th ed.). Eugene: University of Oregon, Institute for the Development of Educational Achievement.

Good, R. H., Simmons, D. C., & Kame'enui, E. J. (2001). The importance and decision-making utility of a continuum of fluency-based indicators of foundational reading skills for third-grade high-stakes outcomes. *Scientific Studies of Reading, 5*(3), 257–288.

Grace, K. (2006). *Phonics and spelling through phoneme-grapheme mapping*. Longmont, CO: Sopris West Educational Services.

Graham, S., Harris, K. R., Fink, B., & MacArthur, C. A. (2001). Teacher efficacy in writing: A construct validation with primary grade teachers. *Scientific Studies of Reading, 5*(2), 177–202.

Greene, J. (2008). *LANGUAGE!* (3rd ed.). Longmont, CO: Sopris West Educational Services.

Hamilton, C., & Shinn, M. R. (2003). Characteristics of word callers: An investigation of the accuracy of teachers' judgments of reading comprehension and oral reading skills. *School Psychology Review, 32*(2), 228–240.

Hart Paulson, L. (in press). *Early childhood* LETRS®. Longmont, CO: Sopris West Educational Services.

Hasbrouck, J., & Denton, C. (2005). *The reading coach: A how-to manual for success*. Longmont, CO: Sopris West Educational Services.

Hasbrouck, J. E., & Tindal, G. A. (2006). Oral Reading Fluency (ORF) norms: A valuable assessment tool for reading teachers. *The Reading Teacher, 59*(7), 636–644.

Hasbrouck, J. E., & Tindal, G. A. (2005). *Oral reading fluency: 90 years of measurement* (BRT Tech. Rep. No. 33). Eugene, OR: University of Oregon, College of Education, Behavioral Research and Teaching. Retrieved July 7, 2008, from http://www.brtprojects.org/techreports/TR_33_NCORF_DescStats.pdf

Heckelman, R. G. (1969). A neurological-impress method of remedial-reading instruction. *Academic Therapy Quarterly, 4*(4), 277–282.

Herman, R. (in revision). *The Herman reading method™*. Longmont, CO: Sopris West Educational Services.

Hiebert, E. H. (2005). The effects of text difficulty on second graders' fluency development. *Reading Psychology, 26*(2), 183–209.

Hiebert, E. H. (2003). *Quick reads*. Parsipanny, NJ: Pearson Learning Group.

Hosp, M. K., & Fuchs, L. S. (2005). Using CBM as an indicator of decoding, word reading, and comprehension: Do the relations change with grade? *School Psychology Review, 34*(1), 9–26.

Hosp, M. K., Hosp, J. L., & Howell, K. W. (2007). *The ABC's of CBM: A practical guide to curriculum-based measurement*. New York: Guilford Press.

Hudson, R., Mercer, C. D., & Lane, H. (2000). *Exploring reading fluency: A paradigmatic overview*. Unpublished manuscript. Gainesville: University of Florida.

Jukes, M. C. H., Vagh, B., & Kim, Y. S. (2006). Developing measures of reading ability and classroom behaviour for use in multi-country evaluations. *World Bank*.

Kame'enui, E. J., & Simmons, D. C. (2001). The role of fluency in reading competence, assessment and instruction: Fluency at the intersection of accuracy and speed. *Scientific Studies of Reading, 5*(3), 203–210.

Katzir, T., Kim, Y., Wolf, M., O'Brien, B., Kennedy, B., Lovett, M., et al. (2006). Reading fluency: The whole is more than the parts. *Annals of Dyslexia, 56*(1), 51–82.

Mathes, P. G., Torgesen, J. K., Allen, S. H., & Allor, I. H. (2001). *First-grade PALS (Peer-assisted learning strategies)*. Longmont, CO: Sopris West Educational Services.

Meisinger, E. B., Schwanenflugel, P. J., Bradley, B. A., & Stahl, S. A. (2004). Interaction quality during partner reading. *Journal of Literacy Research, 36*(2), 111–140.

Meyer, M. (Winter, 2002). Repeated reading: An old standard is revisited and renovated. *Perspectives* (International Dyslexia Association quarterly newsletter), pp. 15–18.

Meyer, M. S., & Felton, R. H. (1999). Repeated reading to enhance fluency: Old approaches and new directions. *Annals of Dyslexia, 49*, 293–306.

Moats, L. C., & Farrell, L. (2007). *Teaching reading essentials*. Longmont, CO: Sopris West Educational Services.

Moats, L. C., & Farrell, L. (2006). *Teaching reading essentials* (TRE): *Video demonstrations of small-group intervention*. Longmont, CO: Sopris West Educational Services.

National Assessment of Educational Progress (NAEP). (2002). *The nation's report card: Reading 2002.* National Center for Education Statistics (NCES). Publication No. 2003521. Retrieved July 7, 2008, from http://nces.ed.gov/pubsearch/pubsinfo. asp?pubid=2003521

National Assessment of Educational Progress (NAEP). (1992). *1992 reading report card for the nation and the states.* National Center for Education Statistics (NCES). Publication No. 93269. Retrieved July 7, 2008, from http://nces.ed.gov/pubsearch/pubsinfo. asp?pubid=93269

National Center for Education Statistics (NCES). (2002.) *Fourth-grade students reading aloud: NAEP 2002 special study of oral reading.* Washington, DC: Author. Publication No. 2006469. Retrieved July 7, 2008, from http://nces.ed.gov/pubsearch/pubsinfo. asp?pubid=2006469

National Institute of Child Health and Human Development (NICHD). (2000). Report of the National Reading Panel. *Teaching children to read: An evidence-based assessment of the scientific research literature on reading and its implications for reading instruction.* Washington, DC: National Institutes of Health (NIH). Retrieved July 7, 2008, from http://www. nationalreadingpanel.org/Publications/summary.htm

Nelson, J. R., Cooper, P., & Gonzalez, J. (2004). *Stepping stones to literacy.* Longmont, CO: Sopris West Educational Services.

Pikulski, J. J., & Chard, D. J. (2005). Fluency: Bridge between decoding and comprehension. *The Reading Teacher, 58,* 510–519.

Samuels, S. J. (1997). The method of repeated readings. *The Reading Teacher, 50,* 76–81.

Samuels, S. J., & Flor, R. F. (1997). The importance of automaticity for developing expertise in reading. *Reading and Writing Quarterly: Overcoming Learning Difficulties, 13,* 107–121.

Scarborough, H. (2001). Connecting early language and literacy to later reading (dis)abilities: Evidence, theory, and practice. In S. B. Neuman & D. K. Dickinson (Eds.), *Handbook of early literacy research* (pp. 97–110). New York: Guilford Press.

Shinn, M. R. (1998). Identifying and defining academic problems: CBM screening and eligibility procedures. In M. R. Shinn (Ed.), *Curriculum-based measurement: Assessing special children* (pp. 90–129). New York: Guilford Press.

Speece, D. L., & Ritchey, K. D. (2005). A longitudinal study of the development of oral reading fluency in young children at risk for reading failure. *Journal of Learning Disabilities, 38*(5), 387–399.

Stahl, S. A., & Heubach, K. (2005). Fluency-oriented reading instruction. *Journal of literacy research, 37,* 25–60.

Stanovich, K. E. (1990). Concepts in developmental theories of reading skill: Cognitive resources, automaticity, and modularity. *Developmental Review, 10,* 72–100.

Stroop, J. R. (1935). Studies of interference in serial verbal reactions. *Journal of Experimental Psychology, 12,* 643–662.

Therrien, W. J., Gormley, S., & Kubina, R. M. (2006). Boosting fluency and comprehension to improve reading achievement. *Teaching Exceptional Children, 38*(3), 22–26.

Therrien, W. J., Wickstrom, K., & Jones, K. (2006). Effect of a combined repeated reading and question generation intervention on reading achievement. *Learning Disabilities Research & Practice, 21*(2), 89–97.

Tihen, L. (2007). Personal communication: Relationships between oral fluency rates and Florida Comprehensive Achievement Test (FCAT) in Lee County, Florida, 2006–2007.

Torgesen, J., Alexander, A. W., Wagner, R., Rashotte, C. A., Voeller, K., Conway, T., et al. (2001). Intensive remedial instruction for children with severe reading disabilities: Immediate and long-term outcomes from two instructional approaches. *Journal of Learning Disabilities, 34*, 33–58.

Torgesen, J., Wagner, R., & Rashotte, C. (1999). *Test of word reading efficiency* (TOWRE). Longmont, CO: Sopris West Educational Services.

Tyler, B., & Chard, D. J. (2000). Using reader's theatre to foster fluency in struggling readers: A twist on the repeated reading strategy. *Reading and Writing Quarterly, 16*, 163–168.

Vellutino, F. R., Tunmer, W. E., Jaccard, J. J., & Chen, R. (2007). Components of reading ability: Multivariate evidence for a convergent skills model of reading development. *Scientific Studies of Reading, 11*(1), 3–32.

Wolf, M. (2003). *RAVE-O: A curriculum for the development of skills in retrieval rate, automaticity, vocabulary elaboration, and orthography.* Medford, MA: Tufts University, Center for Reading and Language Research.

Wolf, M., & Bowers, P. (2000). Special issue: The double-deficit hypothesis. *Journal of Learning Disabilities, 33*(4), 322–324.

Wolf, M., & Denckla, M. B. (2005). *RAN/RAS: Rapid automatized naming and rapid alternating stimulus tests.* Austin, TX: Pro-Ed.

Wolf, M., & Katzir-Cohen, T. (2001). Reading fluency and its intervention. *Scientific Studies of Reading, 5*(3), 211–239.

Worthy, J., & Prater, K. (2002). I thought about it all night: Reader's theatre for reading fluency and motivation. *The Reading Teacher, 56*(3), 294–297.

Wylie, R. E., & Durrell, D. D. (1970). Teaching vowels through phonograms. *Elementary English, 47*, 787–791.

Teacher Resources

Fluency Assessment

Dynamic Indicators of Basic Early Literacy Skills (DIBELS®)
Web site: http://dibels.uoregon.edu
- DIBELS classroom kits and professional development materials are published by Sopris West Educational Services. Web site: http://www.sopriswest.com

AIMSweb® progress monitoring and assessment system
Web site: http://www.edformation.com

Children's Progress Academic Assessment (CPAA)
Web site: http://www.childrensprogress.com

National Center on Student Progress Monitoring
Web site: http://www.studentprogress.org

Reading Fluency Benchmark Assessor and Reading Fluency Progress Monitor
Web site: http://www.readnaturally.com

Fluency Instruction

Curriculum-Based Measurement Warehouse
Web site: http://www.interventioncentral.org/htmdocs/interventions/cbmwarehouse.php

Practicing Basic Skills in Reading: One-Minute Fluency Builders Series (2008) by R. Beck, P. Anderson, and D. Conrad. Longmont, CO: Sopris West Educational Services.
Web site: http://www.sopriswest.com

Read Naturally®, 750 S. Plaza Drive, Suite 100, St. Paul, MN 55120.
Web site: http://www.readnaturally.com
- Selections of graded texts to be used with tape-recorded models of reading accuracy and prosody

Degrees of Reading Power (DRP) BookLink® CD-ROM. Sopris West Educational Services.
Web site: http://www.sopriswest.com
- Index to more than 26,000 book titles with readability levels

Great Leaps Reading (1996) by K. Campbell. Diarmuid, Inc., P.O. Box 357580, Gainesville, FL 32635.
Web site: http://www.greatleaps.com
  • Provides word lists, phrases, and short selections graded for elementary, middle grade, and high school readers

The Six-Minute Solution: A Reading Fluency Program series (2007) by G. Adams and S. Brown. Longmont, CO: Sopris West Educational Services.
Web site: http://www.sopriswest.com
  • Primary, intermediate, and secondary levels

Concept Phonics™ *Speed Drills* by P. Fischer. Oxton House Publishers, P.O. Box 209, Farmington, ME 04938.
Web site: http://www.oxtonhouse.com/reading_speed_drills.html
  • Word, phrase, and text readings sequentially organized to complement most structured, sequential reading programs

Practices for Developing Accuracy & Fluency (grades 1–4). Neuhaus Education Center, 4433 Bissonnet, Bellaire, TX 77401.
Web site: http://www.neuhaus.org

Power Readers (2007) by S. Ebbers. Longmont, CO: Sopris West Educational Services.
Web site: http://www.sopriswest.com
  • Set of 28 related decodable stories with prereading and postreading activity pages (grade K–1 and Intervention K–4)

Spellography: A Student Road Map to Better Spelling (2003) by L. Moats and B. Rosow. Longmont, CO: Sopris West Educational Services.
Web site: http://www.sopriswest.com

Building Fluency: Lessons and Strategies for Reading Success (2001) by W. Blevins. New York: Scholastic.

Answer Key

Chapter 1
The Importance of Fluency in Learning to Read

Warm-Up: World Bank Video (p. 5)

1. Why do you think that 60 words correct per minute (WCPM) was the criterion chosen to represent a minimal level of fluency for second-grade children in Peru?

   Because children who begin school with linguistic, educational, and socioeconomic deficits are at a disadvantage in terms of reading development compared to children in more developed countries, and this level predicts later success in literacy achievement.

2. Why were the children asked to answer questions about what they read?

   To ensure that they were comprehending what they were reading and not simply reading for speed.

3. What did you learn about the children who were learning to read fluently in two languages?

   - **Fluency may transfer from one language to another.**
   - **Fluency in two languages can be developed simultaneously.**

Exercise 1.1: An Experiment in Oral Reading Fluency (p. 11)

The mean of oral reading fluency scores in the group will be approximately 200 WCPM on the *Alice's Adventures in Wonderland* excerpt and between 150–180 WCPM on the *Scientific Studies of Reading* article.

Chapter 2
How Do Children Become Fluent Readers?

Warm-Up: Review Fluency and the Four-Part Processing Model for Word Recognition (p. 15)

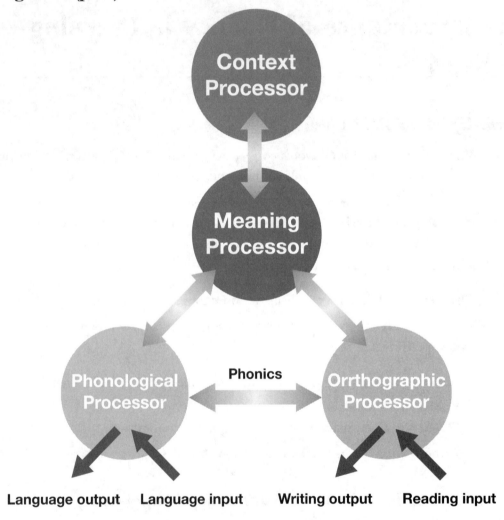

- Explain how fluent word recognition is represented in this model.

  Fluent word recognition is indicated by the bidirectional arrows, which represent neural pathways among the processing systems.

Exercise 2.1: Experience the "Stroop Effect" (p. 21)

1. Was it difficult to name the colors quickly without attending to the words? Why is it easier to read the words than name the colors?

   Most people find that reading printed words is automatic and naming colors in print is very slow and effortful.

2. How does automatic word-reading affect fluency?

   Automatic word-reading allows more attention to be allocated to comprehension, and it facilitates memory for major ideas in the text.

Exercise 2.2: Practice Alphabetic Prosody (p. 27)
(No Answer Key. Responses will vary.)

Exercise 2.3: Phoneme–Grapheme Association (p. 30)

Consonant Phonemes	Grapheme(s)	Word Examples
/p/	p	pat, spa, stomp
/b/	b	but, brought, stubble
/m/	m, mn, mb	milk, bomb, autumn
/t/	t, tt, ed	tent, putt, missed
/d/	d, ed	desk, dress, summed
/n/	n, kn, gn	neck, know, gnaw
/k/	k, c, ck, ch, lk, que, qu	kettle, cot, deck, chorus, talk, unique, quit
/g/	g, gh, gue	get, ghost, fatigue, league
/ng/	ng, n	rang, dank
/f/	f, ff, ph, gh, lf	fine, staff, asphalt, rough, half
/v/	v, ve	very, give
/s/	s, ss, sc, ps	suit, pass, scent, psycho
/z/	z, zz, se, s, x	zen, fuzz, rise, his, xerox
/th/	th	thing, bath, ether

Consonant Phonemes	Grapheme(s)	Word Examples
/<u>th</u>/	th	that, seethe, weather
/sh/	sh, ss, s, ch, sc, ti, si, ci	shawl, pressure, sugar, chagrin, conscious, spatial, mission, special
/zh/	s, z, si, -ge	measure, seizure, vision, rouge
/ch/	ch, tch, tu	cheese, sketch, furniture
/j/	j, dge, ge	judge, page
/l/	l, ll, le	lice, pill, bubble
/r/	r, wr	rat, wrist
/y/	y, (u, eu), i	your, Europe, unique, onion
/w/	w, (q)u	want, question
/wh/	wh	whale
/h/	h, wh	harm, whose

Vowel Phonemes	Grapheme(s)	Word Examples
/ē/	ee, e_e, e, ea, ey, y, ie, ei	see, these, me, eat, key, happy, chief, either
/ĭ/	i, y	it, gym
/ā/	a_e, ai, ay, ea, a, eigh, ei, ey	make, rain, play, great, baby, eight, vein, they
/ĕ/	e, ea	bed, breath
/ă/	a	cat
/ī/	i_e, ie, y, igh, i	time, pie, cry, right, rifle
/ŏ/	o, a, al	fox, swap, palm
/ŭ/	u, o, oo, ough	cup, cover, flood, tough
/aw/	aw, au, al, a, ough	saw, pause, call, water, bought

Vowel Phonemes	Grapheme(s)	Word Examples
/ō/	o_e, oa, oe, ow, o, ough	vote, boat, toe, snow, open, though
/o͝o/	oo, u, oul	took, put, could
/ū/	oo, u_e, ue, ew, ui, ou	moo, tube, blue, chew, suit, soup
/yū/	u_e, ew, u, eu	cute, few, universe, feud
/oi/	oi, oy	oil, boy
/ou/	ou, ow	out, cow
/er/	er, ir, ur	her, sir, fur
/ar/	ar	cart
/or/	or	sport

Take 2 Review: Create a Speed Drill (p. 42)
(No Answer Key. Responses will vary.)

Chapter 3
Improving Fluency in Each Tier of Instruction

Warm-Up: Review Norms for Oral Reading Fluency (ORF) by Grade Level and Reading Level (p. 43)

- Answer these questions in your discussion:

    1. Do students typically lose fluency over the summer months? **Yes**
       - Why might this happen?

         Students may not practice reading during the 2–3 months time away from school.

    2. At what grade levels do gains in fluency level off?

       Gains in fluency begin to level off at fifth grade. By sixth grade, students are almost at the typical adult ORF level.

— What does this suggest in terms of assessment and instruction in reading?

At fifth grade and beyond, only students who are below grade level are likely to need instruction that focuses on fluency development.

3. Select one grade level, and compare a student who is at the 10th percentile with a student at the 90th percentile. If each student reads 10 minutes per day, what might be the approximate difference in the number of words read in a 30-week school year?

A third-grade example: **At the beginning of third grade, a student at the 10th percentile would read 210 words in 10 minutes per day and a student at the 90th percentile would read 1,280 words in 10 minutes per day. In one week (five days), the poor reader would read 1,050 words and the good reader would read 6,400 words—a difference of 5,350 words. In 30 weeks of a school year, that difference balloons to 160,500 words—31,500 words versus 192,000 words. The good reader would probably read many more minutes both inside and outside of school than the poor reader, so she could easily be exposed to 10–12 times as many words in print as the poor reader in a year's time.**

Exercise 3.1: Role-Play and View a Video Demonstration of Partner-Reading (p. 49)

(No Answer Key for role-play portion of this exercise.)

Questions after participants view the video:

1. What does the teacher do to explain the activity?

She role-plays with one student while explaining every guideline.

2. Does the second pair of students know what to do after the explanation?

They were able to carry out their roles and the comprehension check.

3. Would they need more explanation or supervision to maintain appropriate behavior?

They might need additional review and supervision to stay on track.

Exercise 3.2: Practice Phrase-Cued Oral Reading and View a Video Demonstration (p. 56)

(No Answer Key for role-play portion of this exercise.)

Question after participants view the video:

— How does the teacher explain the activity?

She emphasizes sliding words together into groups and reading smoothly, the way we normally speak.

Exercise 3.3: View a Video Demonstration and Role-Play SOR (p. 57)

(No Answer Key for role-play portion of this exercise.)

Questions after participants view the video:

1. What two techniques does the teacher use to make certain the student knows the words in the upcoming text?

   She previews the words in print and discusses each meaning.

2. Does the teacher model and give strategies for increasing speed? Where and how?

   Yes; she uses her finger on the text and her voice to move the student along. She also models the sounds of fluent reading.

Review: Evaluate Fluency in Your Reading Program (p. 60)

(No Answer Key. Responses will vary, depending on participants' core programs.)

Chapter 4
The Measurement of Reading Fluency

Warm-Up: Observe ORF (p. 61)

- View a video of the administration of an ORF assessment.

  - Can you tell if the student was reading fluently, just by listening?

    Yes, because prosody is an indicator of fluency and comprehension. Fluent readers can vocally convey the meaning of a passage to the listener.

  - What enables someone to be a fluent reader?

    Automatic subskills as well as knowledge of the topic, the vocabulary, and the language patterns in a text.

  - Can listening to a person read provide valid and reliable assessment information about reading proficiency?

    Yes, although measurement is advised to verify diagnostic hunches.

Exercise 4.1: Score an ORF Assessment (p. 64)

- DIBELS® (6th ed.) Grade 1 Oral Reading Fluency Passage: **44 WCPM**
- DIBELS® (6th ed.) Grade 6 Benchmark 1.1:   **92 WCPM**

Exercise 4.2: Practice Calculating ORF Percent Accuracy and WCPM (p. 69)

- A student read a third grade passage for 1 minute.
- She read 53 words correctly, and she made 7 errors.

  1. Is the student reading at or near the 50th percentile for third grade?
     No. A WCPM of 53 is between the 25th and 50th percentile for the fall of third grade.

  2. What percentage of words did she read accurately?
     88 percent

  3. How would you summarize this score? Is the student not at risk, at some risk, or at significant risk based on this score?
     Based on both accuracy and WCPM, this student is at some risk and needs intervention.

Exercise 4.3: Chart Progress-Monitoring WCPM Data (p. 70)

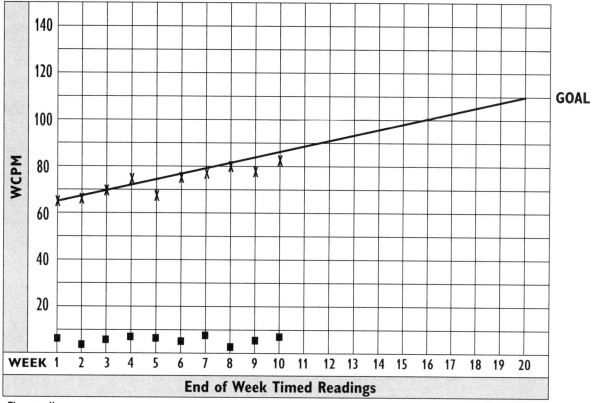

CBM Progress Graph

Time = X   Errors = ■

- Given the trend in these data, does it look as if the instruction is appropriate (i.e., is the student responding to the intervention)?

  Yes, there is steady improvement toward the goal of 92 WCPM, the 50th percentile for mid-grade 3.

- Is the text that is being used for time readings at the right level of difficulty for this student?

  Yes. The student consistently reads between 90–95 percent of the words correctly.

Take 2 Review (p. 73)

- Return to the definition of *reading fluency* that you wrote at the beginning of Chapter 1. Rewrite that definition with any changes you would like to make.

  Answers will vary, but typically may include the addition of emphasis on comprehension.

- At the end of Chapter 1, you posed three questions that you wanted to have answered as you studied this module. Were those questions addressed or are they still unanswered? Write what you have learned about the answers to your questions.

  Questions and answers will vary.

Final Quiz, Module 5 (p. 74)

(Answer Key is provided in the Module 5 Presenter's Kit.)

Index

Note: Page numbers in *italics* refer to the Answer Key.

A

C

J

L

M

N

O

P